Praise for *Between the Spreadsheets*

'Everyone talks about why data is important, but rarely do people bother to talk about how to make data useful, especially if it is dirty. Susan does just that by giving readers very clear and practical details on how to clean, structure, and classify data in a sustainable way. The lessons are clear and imbued with Susan's wit and experience, which makes learning this complex topic fun. This should be a foundational text in all procurement training and university programs.'

**Dr Elouise Epstein,** *Partner at Kearney and author of 'Trade Wars, Pandemics, and Chaos'*

'Only Susan could write a book like this! Dirty data is a problem facing every organisation and Susan takes you step by step through the process for fixing this in a pragmatic, straightforward and simple fashion, but more importantly she brings the subject to life. In this book she perfectly balances being informative with being engaging.'

**Caroline Carruthers,** *Chief Executive of Carruthers and Jackson and bestselling author*

'"Garbage in is garbage out". The world is inundated with data, everyone wants a piece, but how do we make sure the data is usable? Susan Walsh is a leader in this space and has written a wonderful book all should read on dirty data and classifying it correctly. This is both for the preparer, the user, and everyone who is looking to take part in the data revolution.'

**Jordan Morrow,** *the 'Godfather of Data Literacy'*

'Susan's writing style is unique and effective at making the technical data quality topics highly enjoyable to consume. Her brilliant idea of data getting a COAT on is a powerful method for guiding readers through the steps required for protecting your data quality.'

**Kate Strachnyi,** *Founder of DATAcated*

'This book is a page turner. Susan's unique style keeps you engaged and craving to learn more from the practical steps and examples she so carefully presents in this book. This is a must read for both business and data professionals who want to clean up their data and get more out of it.'

**George Firican,** *Founder of LightsOnData and data governance expert*

'Susan Walsh is a force of nature in the data business. She brightens any LinkedIn feed while broadcasting live from her Data Den in front of pink glittery streamers or posting crazy lip-sync videos. In *Between the Spreadsheets*, Susan's vivacious humor and unstoppable spirit livens up an otherwise traditionally boring topic - Data Quality. But inaccurate, inconsistent, untrustworthy data remains a serious problem that plagues literally every company. And Susan can help.

Whether you learn from her practical hands-on tips and tricks or her inspirational life story you're sure to leave with more than you came with (and knowing Susan, probably more than you bargained for!).

So grab a glass of Prosecco, don your Data COAT and slip Between The Spreadsheets to learn how to clean that dirty data of yours, once and for all!'

**Scott Taylor, *The Data Whisperer***

# Between the Spreadsheets

Every purchase of a Facet book helps to fund CILIP's advocacy, awareness and accreditation programmes for information professionals.

# Between the Spreadsheets

## Classifying and Fixing Dirty Data

Susan Walsh

facet
publishing

Published by Facet Publishing
7 Ridgmount Street, London WC1E 7AE
www.facetpublishing.co.uk

Facet Publishing is wholly owned by CILIP: the Library and Information Association.

*British Library Cataloguing in Publication Data*
A catalogue record for this book is available from the British Library.

ISBN 978-1-78330-503-2 (paperback)
ISBN 978-1-78330-504-9 (PDF)
ISBN 978-1-78330-523-0 (EPUB)

First published 2021

Text printed on FSC accredited material.

Typeset from author's files in 10.5/13pt University Old Style and Myriad Pro by Flagholme Publishing Services.
Printed and made in Great Britain by CPI Group (UK) Ltd, Croydon, CR0 4YY.

# Contents

| | | |
|---|---|---:|
| **Figures** | | ix |
| **Tables** | | xi |
| **Acknowledgements** | | xiii |
| **Abbreviations** | | xv |
| **Introduction** | | xvii |
| **1** | **The Dangers of Dirty Data** | **1** |
| | What is dirty data? | 1 |
| | The consequences of dirty data | 5 |
| | How to ensure data accuracy | 11 |
| | How to maintain and spot-check your data | 22 |
| | Conclusion | 34 |
| **2** | **Supplier Normalisation** | **37** |
| | What is supplier normalisation? | 37 |
| | Normalisation best practice and rules | 42 |
| | Normalising suppliers in Excel | 45 |
| | Automating normalisation in Excel | 57 |
| | Conclusion | 59 |
| **3** | **Taxonomies** | **61** |
| | What is a taxonomy? | 61 |
| | Why do I need a taxonomy? Why not use GL codes? | 62 |
| | What is a good/bad taxonomy? | 63 |
| | Off-the-shelf versus custom | 66 |
| | How to build a spend taxonomy | 67 |
| | Conclusion | 68 |
| **4** | **Spend Data Classification** | **69** |
| | What is spend data classification? | 69 |
| | Classification best practice | 70 |
| | Classifying data in Excel | 75 |
| | Updating new data with existing classified data | 89 |
| | Conclusion | 97 |

| | | |
|---|---|---:|
| **5** | **Basic Data Cleansing** | **99** |
| | Cleansing personal data | 99 |
| | Cleansing names in Excel | 99 |
| | Cleansing addresses in Excel | 104 |
| | Conclusion | 109 |
| **6** | **Other Methodologies** | **111** |
| | Alternative tools | 111 |
| | Omniscope | 111 |
| | Artificial intelligence (AI), automation and machine learning (ML) | 126 |
| | Data cleansing tools | 129 |
| | Conclusion | 129 |
| **7** | **The Dirty Data Maturity Model** | **131** |
| | The dirty data maturity model | 131 |
| | Dirty data | 131 |
| | Declassed data | 133 |
| | Distributed data | 134 |
| | Disordered data | 135 |
| | Dirt-free data | 137 |
| | Conclusion | 138 |
| **8** | **Data Horror Stories** | **139** |
| | Scenario: Edinburgh children's hospital | 139 |
| | Scenario: Ted Baker | 140 |
| | Stories of the common data people | 141 |
| | Final thoughts | 149 |
| | **Summary** | **151** |
| | Dirty data | 151 |
| | COAT | 151 |
| | Normalisation | 152 |
| | Taxonomies | 152 |
| | Data classification | 152 |
| | Data cleansing | 152 |
| | Data tools | 153 |
| | Data maintenance | 153 |
| | And, of course, the horror stories | 153 |
| | **References** | **155** |
| | **Index** | **157** |

# Figures

| | | |
|---|---|---|
| 1.1 | Pivot table initial layout | 24 |
| 1.2 | Changing pivot table format to Tabular Form | 25 |
| 1.3 | Updated pivot table layout | 26 |
| 1.4 | Removing Grand Totals from a pivot table | 27 |
| 1.5 | Checking for classification errors in the pivot table | 28 |
| 1.6 | Selecting a new window | 30 |
| 1.7 | How to Arrange All views vertically | 31 |
| 1.8 | Views arranged vertically | 32 |
| 1.9 | Example of blank spaces in pivot table | 33 |
| 1.10 | How to Repeat All Item Labels in pivot | 34 |
| 1.11 | Pivot table with All Item Labels repeated | 35 |
| 2.1 | Normalised versus Un-normalised suppliers | 41 |
| 2.2 | Using the UPPER formula | 43 |
| 2.3 | Copying the cell by dragging down | 43 |
| 2.4 | Pasting values | 44 |
| 2.5 | Using the TRIM formula | 45 |
| 2.6 | Example of multiple spaces | 45 |
| 2.7 | Using the RIGHT formula | 46 |
| 2.8 | Results of using the RIGHT formula | 47 |
| 2.9 | Example of Inc in a supplier name | 48 |
| 2.10 | Hiding rows | 48 |
| 2.11 | What happens when you copy and paste cells while on a filter | 49 |
| 2.12 | An alternative way to copy cells while on a filter | 49 |
| 2.13 | Dragging the formula down and the results | 49 |
| 2.14 | Search and replace | 50 |
| 2.15 | An alternative to the RIGHT formula | 51 |
| 2.16 | Pivot of normalised suppliers | 54 |
| 2.17 | Adding a new window and arranging it vertically | 54 |
| 2.18 | Arranged view vertically | 55 |
| 2.19 | Using a VLOOKUP formula | 56 |
| 2.20 | Results of using the VLOOKUP formula | 57 |
| 2.21 | Aggregated supplier and normalised name using a pivot | 58 |
| 4.1 | Aggregated supplier and classifications in a pivot | 87 |
| 4.2 | COUNTIF formula | 91 |
| 4.3 | Results of copying the formula down | 91 |
| 4.4 | Filtering on unique classifications | 92 |

| | | |
|---|---|---|
| 4.5 | VLOOKUP for updating new data with existing classified data | 93 |
| 4.6 | How the data should look with VLOOKUP applied | 93 |
| 4.7 | Applying a CONCATENATE formula | 95 |
| 4.8 | How the data should look when the CONCATENATE | 95 |
| | formula is applied | 96 |
| 4.9 | Using a VLOOKUP on the concatenated data | 96 |
| 4.10 | How the VLOOKUP data should look | 96 |
| 5.1 | Sample of personal data | 100 |
| 5.2 | Using the CONCATENATE formula to merge the first name | 103 |
| | and middle name | |
| 5.3 | Using a VLOOKUP to pull through the correctly formatted addresses | 107 |
| 6.1 | How to open Omniscope from a file saved in a folder | 112 |
| 6.2 | Selecting the right option to open the file | 113 |
| 6.3 | How to open a file from within Omniscope | 114 |
| 6.4 | Options when opening an Excel file with multiple tabs | 114 |
| 6.5 | Loading the block in Omniscope | 115 |
| 6.6 | Inserting a new field in Omniscope | 115 |
| 6.7 | Using the Keep button | 117 |
| 6.8 | Using the text search filter | 118 |
| 6.9 | Results of filtering the data | 119 |
| 6.10 | Using the category filter | 121 |
| 6.11 | Using a data model to merge files | 123 |
| 6.12 | Using the Merge/Join box | 125 |
| 6.13 | Using the Merge/Join box with multiple criteria | 126 |
| 7.1 | The dirty data maturity model | 131 |

# Tables

| | | |
|---|---|---|
| 2.1 | Common supplier names | 38 |
| 2.2 | Words and letters on the risky list | 42 |
| 2.3 | Master search list | 52 |
| 3.1 | Example of a simple taxonomy | 62 |
| 3.2 | Options for a Level 1 taxonomy | 64 |
| 3.3 | Examples of poor and good descriptions | 66 |
| 4.1 | Examples of invoice line descriptions | 71 |
| 4.2 | A supplier viewed as an individual row | 72 |
| 4.3 | A supplier viewed with all their rows | 72 |
| 4.4 | Classification errors involving delivery | 73 |
| 4.5 | Classification errors involving maintenance | 73 |
| 4.6 | Common words and companies found when classifying spend data | 76 |
| 4.7 | Suppliers with a specific classification | 79 |
| 4.8 | Examples of deceptive descriptions | 82 |
| 4.9 | Examples of descriptions with suggested classifications | 83 |
| 4.10 | Common typos | 85 |
| 4.11 | Common abbreviations in MRO | 86 |

# Acknowledgements

Firstly, I have to thank my dad, Bill, my biggest supporter, who has helped me through some really tough times without ever wavering in his support or love. And he still continues to give me advice, knowing that I probably won't take it. Love you lots.

Then there's my brother Will. He's the voice of reason sitting on my shoulder asking 'is that wise?' He and his wife Kristianne (and not forgetting Rocco the dog) have been great cheerleaders when things have been tough and I thank you all for that greatly. Love you guys.

And then there's my mum, Joan, who's no longer with us. She would have been so unbelievably proud and the whole of Dundee would have known about this book before it had even been written. But she'd also be very disappointed I've not been married off yet. I hope this makes up for it, Mum, miss you and love you loads.

Next, it has to be Vicki Connor. A straight-talking, no-nonsense coach who metaphorically pulled me off the road at the last minute before a truck of destruction hit. She never took advantage when I was down and did quite the opposite – lifted me up higher than ever before. With her coaching, my mindset and self-belief has changed for the better and I don't think I'd even have considered writing this book without her subconscious ninja mind tricks.

Followed closely behind is Michelle Henty and Helena Jannson West. My bestest friends in the whole world who have peeled me off the floor when things have been down, or off the ceiling when life's been good. Your support has been invaluable and we've kept the Prosecco industry alive in the last few years. I look forward to sharing many more Proseccos with you both.

None of this would have been possible had it not been for a chat with Caroline Carruthers, who believed in me enough to introduce me to my now publisher, Peter Baker at Facet Publishing. You both saw the potential I knew was there and I thank you both for seeing that and embracing the crazy.

Then there are the book reviewers, the ones who gave honest and constructive feedback. Thank you so much Natalie, Kavita, Kirsty, Danielle, Kate, George, Michelle, Adriana and Edward.

To Ferdos, Sarah, Tracey and Tiff, my oldest friends – thank you for being there, always.

Kay and Eric, you've been cheering me right on too, even though you have no idea what I do. The best kind of family.

The legend that is Scott Taylor, the Data Whisperer, can't go without recognition. He welcomed me into his group, showcased me to the world through 'The 12 Days of Data Management', and through him I got to know Kate Strachnyi and George Firican. We've been firm friends ever since, despite the distance. I'm so lucky to know you guys.

To my procurement ladies, in particular Sarah, Sarah and Amanda. Thank you for your support and friendship, you inspire me every day.

Finally, to every single follower and connection on LinkedIn, I thank you. You've embraced my unique style and given me so much fun and joy. Thank you.

I know I've probably forgotten someone, so please use this as your acknowledgement!

# Abbreviations

| | |
|---|---|
| AI | Artificial Intelligence |
| B2B | Business to Business |
| B2C | Business to Consumer |
| CIPS | The Chartered Institute of Procurement & Supply |
| COAT | Consistent, Organised, Accurate, Trustworthy |
| CPO | Chief Procurement Officer |
| DPO | Data Protection Officer |
| EEA | European Economic Area |
| EU | European Union |
| EUR | Euro |
| GBP | British Pound Sterling |
| GDPR | The General Data Protection Regulation |
| GL | General Ledger |
| HR | Human Resources |
| HVAC | Heating, Ventilation and Air Conditioning |
| ICO | Information Commissioners Office |
| ML | Machine Learning |
| MRO | Maintenance, Repair and Operations |
| PO | Purchase Order |
| RFID | Radio Frequency ID |
| RPA | Robotic Process Automation |
| SKU | Stock Keeping Unit |
| UNSPSC | United Nations Standard Products and Services Code |
| USA | United States of America |
| USD | United States Dollar |

# Introduction

Hello and welcome to *Between the Spreadsheets: Classifying and Fixing Dirty Data.*

This is not your typical data book and that's because I'm not your typical data person. I have a wonderfully unique background that's a mix of corporate and data work, which has brought me to the point where I'm able to share my specialist knowledge with you.

Regardless of whether you are completely intimidated by data, starting out in your data career, a seasoned procurement or data professional, or a decision maker within an organisation, there will be something in here for you.

Dirty data is a problem. In every single organisation, no matter how big or small or where they're located, you will hear talk of data quality issues. What you will rarely hear about is the consequences of this because people or companies don't want to admit their failures. We could be talking about millions of pounds or dollars lost on new technology, weeks or months spent fixing mistakes due to bad data, possible job losses or even worse.

It's not just that. We hear all the time of data scientists spending anything from 40-80% of their time cleaning or wrangling data. Why is this? Well, I believe it's because they are inefficient and inexperienced at it. 'What? But they're data scientists!' I hear you cry. Unfortunately, that doesn't mean anything. Data cleaning is rarely covered in academic studies or other courses; the focus is always on the technical aspects of the role, yet ironically, they can't do any of that without the clean data first.

While data cleaning is one of the most vital parts of the whole process when working with data, it is often overlooked because either there is an assumption that people already know how to do it or it's considered too menial or not important enough to spend time on, or invest in.

It's not just in data science; I've seen this in other areas. I was managing a politics student and asked her to book a meeting and send invites. When it hadn't been done, I asked why and she explained she didn't know how to do it. I was blown away that someone studying politics (don't ask me why the politics thing made a difference, I have no idea) didn't know how to create a meeting invite. My assumptions were very wrong.

Then there was the time when I was in a new role and being trained by someone in his late twenties, at least ten years younger than me. He was using right-click to cut and paste all the data in his spreadsheet, so I showed him the shortcut of ctrl+c to copy and ctrl+v to paste. Can you imagine the amount of time he must have spent right-clicking? All those seconds throughout a day add up over the course of a year, plus it must have been hard on his hand doing all that repetitive clicking.

If you thought that was the story, well you're in for a treat. When we finished that training session, he said to me 'and just click this x in the corner to save'. I am not kidding. I put my hands up to my face in horror as he told me this. My very core was shaking, I had cold sweats and I made him promise never to do that ever again. Can you imagine if he lost his work? That's all hours or days of work lost to the business. Thankfully, we have autosave now, but there are still occasions when this doesn't work properly and you shouldn't just take it for granted.

There is a huge gap between what industry assumes or expects of students and what their skill levels are. I want to raise this as an issue to be aware of and use this book to help. Even *The Guardian* (2021) has reported that there's a sharp fall in the number of people taking IT courses. Why is this? Well, let's face it, data can be a very dry and boring subject. (Except when you talk to me of course. I have a data den with pink glittery streamers and do lip-sync videos on LinkedIn.)

I am everything that you don't expect someone working in data to be. And that is a very good thing. It's also why I have a fun book title: I want non-data people to see the title and consider reading this. I want this book to be seen by young people as an opportunity to have fun with data, to see that you can make of it what you want and be who you want and still do a great job while educating people on how to have better data.

It's not just the young people looking to enter into data that struggle with a skill gap; I often hear stories of graduates getting their first jobs in an organisation and being handed their first 'real' data set and they don't know what to do with it. They have been used to working with sterile data sets in a test environment in academia and they don't know how to deal with a real live working data set because they've never seen one in context before.

As procurement moves toward digitisation, there are data quality issues prohibiting this. It wouldn't be a stretch to assume that a mixture of lack of skill and lack of investment in these areas is at least causing some of these data quality issues.

*The Deloitte Global Chief Procurement Officer Survey 2019* found that 60% of Chief Procurement Officers (CPOs) stated poor master data quality, standardisation and governance as the biggest challenge for mastering digital complexity. 57% said that the quality and accessibility of data presented strong barriers to technology adoption. These are all things I will address in this book.

I want to highlight that clean data is an investment, not a cost, and I want to demonstrate exactly how much of an investment it is - you could be saving so much more than just time and money. You don't have to invest in super expensive consultants or some fancy software; it can be done in Excel. It might not always be the most efficient way, but for those with limited budgets, it is a way.

I'm here to tell you that it's really, really, *really* important to have good data quality and that if you or your team are not experienced in this area, get reading! Not only will it help make your job easier, but it could potentially save you bucketloads of time and money and give you peace of mind. Now, isn't that worth it?

I think it's important that from the top to the bottom of an organisation, every single person should understand the impact of dirty data and how to spot it. In this book, I'm going to explain why and show you how.

After reading this, not only will you be able to work with your data more efficiently, but you'll also understand the impact that the work you do with it has and how it affects the rest of the organisation, including your colleagues.

Before we get into the nuts and bolts of this, let's answer what will probably be your first question: who is Susan Walsh, The Classification Guru, and what makes her qualified to talk about this?

Let's start at the beginning of my career. I'd never really known what I wanted to do or felt like I had a calling. I decided to study for a degree in Commerce as I thought it would cover many areas and that I would definitely know what I wanted to do when I graduated. Guess what? I didn't.

I grew up in a place called Broughty Ferry in Dundee, Scotland, where the main career options were retail or call centres and I knew those weren't for me. When I graduated, I got a job as a paint merchandiser and that company moved me down to Guildford in England, where I still live 20 years later. But, as you may have already guessed, that job did not last.

For the remainder of my twenties, I tried out a number of careers that mainly revolved around sales. Sales rep, telesales executive, account manager, national account executive and national account manager. All within large blue-chip companies, working with some well known retailers.

Somewhere along the way, I realised I was doing what I *thought* I should be doing, rather than what I *wanted* to do, even though I still didn't know what that was. Then I had an idea: 'let's open a shop!' It was at a time when working in the corporate world was changing for women. It was less suit and blouse and more smart/casual, pretty dresses and tops. Online retail hadn't really taken off yet and it was harder to source nice clothing, so I decided to open a shop. In Guildford. One of the most expensive towns in the UK for commercial rent.

However, I was confident. I had designed a beautiful shop with lovely clothing at a reasonable price . . . and it bombed. Months and months went by with a few customers here and there. Some days no one came in at all. It was soul-destroying. In my gut, I knew it wouldn't work, but I tried to hang on for as long as possible.

What I could never have planned for was the level of brand snobbery in my town. If it wasn't Chanel or Gucci, they weren't interested. I had people walk by for months before they would be comfortable even stepping foot in my shop. It was so hard. At one point, I had a return of an item after Christmas and I barely had enough money to refund the customer – it was really tough.

'This is all very interesting, but what does this have to do with the book?' I hear you say. Well, the next part is where my data journey began.

I had literally no money. I couldn't even afford to go bankrupt. I had to get a job to save up and pay for it. I was desperate for work and I found an online ad for some data entry work for a Spend Analytics company. Although I had never worked in Procurement or Data, I thought I'd be good at it as I had worked for many corporates and knew what they were buying and how their budgets worked, but more than that, I just needed a job. Little did I know how good I would actually be at that job and, more importantly, how much I'd enjoy it.

I found that classifying data came very naturally to me. I understood the context of how the data was being spent, which in the spend data world is not always what it seems to be. (But I'll get into that later.)

I also had to work with a number of analysts, which opened up a whole new world of different languages and communication that was different from what I was used to in the corporate world. After some time working in that environment, I was able to understand both perspectives and become a translator of sorts between the two worlds.

Five happy years followed, and, as the business grew, so did my responsibilities. By the end, I was managing a team of 14 who I'd recruited, trained and managed myself. Through that, I learned how to train and share my knowledge and processes with my team.

Eventually, I needed to move on and find new challenges. I knew I wanted to do that within a similar role, but since I had not come from a procurement or data background and I didn't code or have the experience to find a job as a data analyst, I didn't know where I could find a similar role elsewhere. I decided to start my second business – The Classification Guru.

I wanted to be different and unique. I wanted to be myself in all its bubbly craziness. I didn't want to just replicate what my previous company and many others had done or be another boring data person. I wanted to focus on the one big area I could see was being neglected - **spend data classification and data quality**.

I knew that spend data classification had always been offered as part of another service, such as dashboards and analytics, or if a new system or software was purchased, but it was never available as a standalone service. The perception in the industry was always around the value of the software and the analytics, not the cleaning and preparation of the data. Having spent many years tidying up messy data, I could see that the true value was in the quality of the data, yet no one seemed to be speaking about it.

I started talking about it. A lot. To anyone who would listen. Without a single connection in the procurement or data world, I went out and networked, exhibited and used social media to spread my message. I quickly discovered that not just procurement spend data quality but all data quality was an issue and that it was, and still is, a struggle to raise its profile within organisations. Let's face it, it's not the most exciting topic and it intimidates a lot of people. It can be seen as menial work with little value, when in fact it drives everything an organisation does, from cost savings and efficiencies to production and planning to detecting fraudulent activity.

I saw an opportunity to make it more fun and interesting. Yes, it's a serious subject with some highly skilled and knowledgeable people working in the industry, but they are the ones who already know and understand the issues that organisations face with data quality. The people who need to be engaged are the ones in the rest of the organisation, the ones working with the data, from the receptionist to the planners and forecasters, sales, marketing and supply chain, to the senior executives using the data to make critical business decisions. It needs to be more interesting to be relatable.

To some, it can seem complex and intimidating. Those people very rarely understand the importance of the accuracy of the data they are working with, how it's used or the consequences of when it goes wrong.

That's why I'm writing this book. Whether you have never been interested in data and find it daunting, you're a seasoned professional who is looking to refine or reaffirm your skills, or you're a senior decision maker who wants to understand the impact of dirty data and the value to your organisation, then this book is for you.

I will take you through my definition of dirty data - what is it and what the consequences are of how this affects the rest of the organisation. I'll also show how you can help ensure data accuracy using my COAT methodology, plus the importance of keeping that data COAT on with regular maintenance and spot-checking.

I'll then take you through how to classify, cleanse and normalise, firstly in Excel, as that's a global tool that is accessible to everyone and can be followed by any reader, regardless of skill level or experience. Screenshots and examples will help take you through the processes. This will be followed by me sharing some of my tips with you on how I classify in a different tool and then I'll explore other classification and cleansing options.

If that's not enough, I'll present to you my dirty data maturity model. Yes, it exists and you can gauge where you are and look at steps on how you can improve your dirty data. Finally, I will share with you some data horror stories – there's nothing like finishing up with some drama and suspense, but with a twist!

# 1 The Dangers of Dirty Data

## What is dirty data?

Let's start on some common ground. What exactly is dirty data?

Well, the truth is that it can mean different things to different people working with different types of data. For the purposes of this book, it will be based on information used in a business context.

At its most basic level, dirty data is anything incorrect. It could be things such as:

### Misspelt names

This happens more than you think. If it's supplier names, it could be a simple switch of letters from ABC Printing to ABC Printign, a missing letter such as T Shoesmit instead of T Shoesmith, or something much more subtle like AT Jones, instead of TA Jones, which may not be easily picked up.

If you're dealing with personal information, it's doubly important to get the name right because of data protection regulations, such as the General Data Protection Regulation (GDPR). Very recently, I received a piece of mail for my new limited company 'The Classification Guru Ltd'. The address was correct and my first and middle names were correct, but I had someone else's surname and a business name that wasn't mine.

When I checked on Companies House, I could see that the surname and the business name were related to one person - everything else was my information. What I suspect happened in this instance is one of several things: firstly that the list of names for mailings was in Excel and someone possibly hadn't filtered all columns and the information was therefore mixed up. Secondly, it could have been that some lines of data were removed, which caused some of the information in certain columns to shift up or down and misalign. It could have been something as simple as a cut and paste error that caused the problem. This could have easily been rectified by applying some spot checks to the data before it was used as a mailing list. I'll cover this further later.

## Incorrect or misleading descriptions

In the work I do, I see this a lot in invoice or Purchase Order (PO) descriptions. It could be something as simple as 'services' in the description and the person's name as the supplier. Well, who are they? The copywriter, the lawyer, another consultant of some sort? It can be very tricky to find this out and so, more often than not, it will end up being classified under 'Professional Services'. What if it's actually plumbing or electrical services and should therefore sit under 'Facilities'? It might be a small value, but what if it's not? It could be a large amount of spend that is not being accounted for correctly.

Misleading descriptions in spend data can happen easily if the data is not viewed in context. For example, if you only look at the information in the invoice or PO line description column, but not the supplier name, this can lead to misclassification. You might have 'cleaning' as a description, but the supplier is Dell or IBM. This completely changes the context of the information from janitorial services to data or computer or data cleaning services.

I once trained up a new team member and they classified LinkedIn, that well known business networking platform, as a restaurant because the description said restaurant. They had not viewed the data in context. The true nature of the spend would be more likely a job advertisement for a restaurant related position, or perhaps some advertising for something restaurant related, or even training in something restaurant related.

The spend was large. Had this not been picked up, there could have been thousands of pounds of spend against a restaurant in 'Travel' instead of sitting under 'Marketing'. That's where value can also help guide the classification process, which I'll discuss further in Chapter 4 - Spend Data Classification.

Attention to detail is also key. A large part of the spend data classification process is keyword searches and I'll cover this later, but when you have descriptions such as 'hotel cab' or 'taxi from restaurant to hotel' you have to be careful to read the data correctly and not just assume that because a word is in the description, that is the correct option to classify.

It could also be a completely incorrect description. Images are tagged to appear in searches, but what if a cat is tagged as a dog or vice versa? If you are a business and it's your products that are being tagged incorrectly, then how will your clients or consumers find your products?

If you're a retailer and you sell your products online, what if they're not categorised correctly? I've experienced this myself where I've seen a product I've liked, but when I've tried to find it again by keyword searches, I haven't been able to find it. I've had to literally scroll through ALL the products and who can be bothered with that?

Then there are the GL (General Ledger) codes. These are used by finance departments to account for financial transactions, but unlike spend data classification where the spend is classified exactly as what it is, GL codes can be used to track an item or a project.

A great example is a client of mine who had their data classified for the first time. Once finished, they had visibility on their spend across the whole business globally, including car leasing. When we looked at one particular supplier, the whole classification was car leasing, but there were four different GL codes assigned, ranging from office supplies to employee benefits. From an accounting perspective, this could potentially be correct, however, from a procurement perspective, this information could be misleading during the decision-making process and lead to bad business decisions. It flagged an issue in the finance department where multiple people had been assigning different codes to the same supplier based on their perception of what it should be. I have a solution for this, which I'll get on to later.

## Missing or incorrect codes

This can be a real issue in the manufacturing and supply chain industries. There are several reasons why a product code might be missing. If it's an older product then historically it might never have been assigned a code. Or perhaps the code wasn't available when the product was set up, but no one followed up to add it in once the code had been created.

Then there's the 'can't be bothered' aspect. We don't like to think about it, but some people just can't be bothered to find out the information they need and if they're not being monitored and know they can get away with it, they'll continue to set up products with missing information. It could be wider than just the product code, it could be dimensions and weights, which are critical to many different areas of the business.

Just as harmful to the business is an incorrect code. It could be that a code has been mistyped with some numbers mixed up or perhaps one number or letter missing, or it could be something more subtle like a zero being replaced with the letter O. This can all result in duplicate records for these products, the wrong items being ordered, shipped, manufactured or the number inaccurately reported in inventory, etc., resulting in unnecessary expenditure for the business.

## No standard formats for addresses

I see this a lot in both supplier and personal data. There are multiple ways that an address can be recorded; sometimes it's all in one cell, sometimes split over a number of columns, and I've seen cities in the county or state column, or the postal or zip code in the city or county column. It's a mess and is there to some degree in nearly every data set.

Abbreviations are also problematic: Terrace could be Terr, Place - Plc, Road - Rd, Street - St. This can lead to near-duplicates, multiple records and information split between these multiple records, causing incorrect information and reporting to be used in the business.

## No standard units of measure

This can cause a lot of issues, especially if you are trying to analyse or report on a specific product.

The list below shows common variants found in the data:

- Litre: litres, liter, liters, 1l, 1 l, 1ltr, 1 ltr, 2ltrs, 2 ltrs
- Metre: metres, meter, meters, 1m, 1 m, 1mtr, 1 mtr, 2mtrs, 2 mtrs
- Centimetre: centimetres, centimeter, centimeters, cm, cms, 1cm, 1 cm, 2cms, 2 cms
- Kilometre: kilometres, kilometer, kilometers, km, kms, 1km, 1 km, 2kms, 2 kms
- Gram: grams, gramme, grammes, gm, gms, 1gm, 1 gm, 2gms, 2 gms
- Kilogram: kilograms, kilo, kilos, 1kg, 1 kg, 2kgs, 2kgs
- Pound: pounds, 1lb, 1 lb, 2lbs, 2 lbs.

Even the little things, like whether you decide to have a space between the number and the unit of measure, can cause near duplications. It's much better to be clear and specific with your team to avoid multiple versions of the same items. If you have a global data set, are you working in the same units of measure or do you need to create a conversion to measure or compare like for like? This also leads us on nicely to the next section - currency.

## Currency issues

If you are not aware that the values you are working with are in multiple currencies, you could spend hours trying to get figures to match up. Trust me, I've been there! In particular, when working with something like Swedish Krona versus GBP or USD, the values are significantly higher, so it could end up looking like you've spent £500 on a taxi.

### Incorrect/partially classified spend data

For me, this is worse than not having classified data at all. When clients come to me for help, if they already have classified data, I immediately disregard everything and start again from scratch. Firstly, they wouldn't be using my services if there wasn't an issue with their classified data, and, secondly, in terms of time and being efficient, it's far easier to start again with a clean slate to which you can apply standards that will be consistent and accurate.

### Duplicates

The dreaded duplicates. These can appear in many forms, from duplicate invoices to customer/supplier records, to orders, to products and much more. They cause multiple records, which could mean the information is split, resulting in you only seeing part of the picture. Then there are the *near-duplicates*; don't even get me started on those. In business, this could be PWC/P.W.C., or with personal information, Robert Smith and Bob Smith. I cover this in more detail in the next section.

## The consequences of dirty data

Why does it matter if data isn't quite right? Who's going to notice? Like any problem, it's manageable when it's small, but gone unnoticed or left to fester, it can become a really big issue. What if your car started making a rattling noise? You wouldn't leave that to deteriorate, would you? You definitely wouldn't go on a long road trip and risk being stranded in the middle of nowhere. Likewise, you shouldn't be making big business decisions based on unclassified, poor quality data.

Let's go back to the examples we've just covered. What's the worst that can happen?

### Misspelt names

If names are misspelt, you could have multiple accounts for the same supplier and you could, for example, have some orders being placed under one account and some under the other.

When it comes to running reports, it means you may only be seeing half the picture if you've only selected one of the customers/suppliers. This could have a knock-on effect on areas like forecasting (not planning enough), discounts applied to orders (not giving the customer the correct discount), account management (not being given the right level of service for the amount purchased), sales (forecasting, analytics) and finance (the wrong credit limit, restrictions on purchases).

It's the same for procurement. If you're monitoring supplier spend and you have multiple versions, you don't get a full picture of what you're buying from that supplier and that could impact negotiations, contract compliance and planning. It also means you have fewer suppliers on your system than you think. If you're working with global data sets, this can be a significant difference. A project I recently worked on had 41,000 suppliers in the file, but when I normalised them (more on that in Chapter 2), the true number of suppliers was 34,900. That's a difference of over 6,000 suppliers. If you're working on a supplier rationalisation project, you want to make sure you're working with the correct numbers.

### Incorrect or misleading descriptions

This happens a lot in spend data classification. There are a number of 'deceptive descriptions', such as dues, subscriptions, rent or security, that could mislead the classification of the data if it is not viewed in context with the rest of the file. What does this mean? If you have misclassified high value spend, you could be making bad business decisions and this could be costly.

The same applies to product descriptions: if the descriptions are too vague, the wrong product could be ordered, or shipped, incurring costs or holding up business processes.

### Missing or incorrect codes

If codes are missing or incorrect, are the right products being ordered so that the business can run smoothly? What's the cost to the business of any hold-ups? Or what if the wrong product is picked and shipped to the customer? What is the cost of collecting the return and shipping out a new product? If this happens on multiple items before the issue is picked up, consider the total cost of this error, not only financially, but in time spent by all parties resolving the issue, re-picking and packing the correct items, and shipping them out. These are rarely measured.

### No standard formats for addresses

How much damage could this do? You could end up with duplicate records with the data in different formats, and even different languages. You could find multiple versions of the same address based on the language they are entered in, for example, one city could be Geneva (English), Genève (French), Ginevra (Italian), Genf (German) and Genebra (Portuguese). It's the same for countries, so make sure there's an agreed language in place. Otherwise, and as previously mentioned, this means unnecessary mailings, extra costs and potential duplication of work, for example, by different sales teams both targeting the same prospect.

In addition to that, without standard formats, it makes finding information harder, which in turn can add time onto someone's process when trying to do their work. You might think, well it's only a few minutes, what does that matter? If you add up all those minutes per record, per employee working on them, over a year, those minutes can quickly become days or even weeks of wasted time and a cost to your business.

## No standard units of measure

This can cause all kinds of problems, especially if you are working with global data. A project I worked on for a client in Europe involved rationalising their SKU (Stock Keeping Unit) list. They had hundreds of hubs that were creating their own product descriptions and SKUs, resulting in many versions of the same product. This meant they couldn't track exactly what was being bought centrally and how much of it.

I saw 'litres' spelt multiple different ways, correctly and incorrectly, which created multiple versions of the same product. I started with 32,400 SKUs and managed to rationalise this down to 26,100 by standardising the format of many of the products. This resulted in the client being able to find several areas for cost savings where the hubs were buying from non-approved suppliers at a higher price than the preferred supplier.

## Currency issues

Probably less of an issue, but still an issue nonetheless if gone unnoticed. If a currency conversion hasn't been applied (USD, EUR, GBP are common), you could potentially be reporting massively inflated numbers, which in turn could drive decisions in the business such as growth, budgets and pricing.

## Incorrect/partially classified spend data

In spend data classification things can get messy. There are two common issues I find with existing classified spend data: firstly, there's a lot that's incorrectly classified and secondly, the suppliers are only partially classified (which technically could also be incorrect).

If there is incorrectly classified data, this can mislead procurement teams as to how much they are spending in a particular category or with a particular supplier. The top 80% of spend tends to be checked and focused on, so there is less chance of large errors in this area, but there can be plenty of opportunities to find misclassified data in the bottom 20% (which can be tens or hundreds of thousands of rows of data) and this is known as tail spend.

According to the Chartered Institute of Procurement & Supply (CIPS) (2021), tail spend can often be referred to as 'rogue spend or maverick spend, [and] is usually small value purchases that are conducted by the organisations outside of a contract and often outside of the awareness of the procurement team'. I prefer to explain things in simple terms so, put very plainly, tail spend is mostly all the low-value, fiddly suppliers you've only ever used once (but shouldn't have) and will probably never use again. The issue with tail spend is that it is often neglected as it's very time-consuming to classify, analyse and maintain, and so more often than not the quality is left to decay to the point it is unusable.

There are massive cost-saving opportunities in the tail spend. Think of a bottle of shower gel; there's always a little bit left at the bottom that you can't get out. This is no big deal but imagine over the course of a year if you saved up all those little bits of shower gel that were left, you could probably have another bottle of shower gel. My point is that tail spend is exactly the same. There are lots of opportunities in the tail spend to make significant savings. All those low-value line items can add up to some large amounts, but if they're classified incorrectly, or not classified at all, those cost savings will never be found.

Tail spend can hide other things too. For example, you might not know how many suppliers you have for a specific product or service and this can be important. For one of my clients, I classified 4,000 suppliers from 90 countries in almost as many languages, with just a supplier name and the country they were based in. I won't lie, this was not a fun project, but the outcome was rewarding. The client identified 1,000 consultants from their data, a number far too high, and so they initiated a project to rationalise those consultants. I'm very sure that many of the consultancies on that list were providing the same or similar services that could be channelled through one supplier, negotiated at a better rate.

There are other benefits to rationalising the number of suppliers. There are hidden costs in having so many suppliers, such as the cost of processing invoices. In some cases, the cost of processing the invoice could be more than the value of the invoice itself; what if a supplier is raising multiple invoices each month, what is the cost to your business for that? Without accurate classification and normalisation of the spend data, you won't have the visibility to know this.

While most of these opportunities will be found in the tail spend, sometimes it is the top 80% of suppliers that have dirty spend data. Even if it's just one or two lines incorrectly classified, because the values are so much higher this can have a real impact on reporting and decision making.

A good example of a large, high-spend company found in many spend data sets is IBM, that well known technology company. Typically, within this supplier, you would expect to see spend such as hardware, software and maintenance services. However, on one occasion there was a file that IBM classified as cleaning services. Now, this might be easy to spot if you are looking at the supplier in isolation and all of its rows of data, but when you have thousands, if not millions, of rows, this might not immediately stand out. If you're not looking at your spend data regularly then it's even harder to spot.

What does this mean? Well, suddenly you have x amount of spend misclassified as cleaning and with a supplier such as IBM these values are unlikely to be low. This means you are reporting a potentially large overspend under cleaning services and an underspend in IT, which could have a knock-on effect on things like planning, budgets and supplier negotiations.

## Duplicates

Duplicates can have far-reaching consequences. It doesn't just mean you have multiple versions of the same item or that you don't have true visibility of what you are buying/selling/using. The number of hours that your organisation is wasting in any given week trying to fix problems that have occurred due to duplicates can be large, costly and unseen.

It's rarely measured and so it's hard to quantify, but if you ask some of your colleagues I'm sure you can start to form a picture. By reducing the number or duplicates, you can become more efficient, which leads to higher productivity, reduced costs resulting from errors and even more profitability.

## Other consequences of dirty data

These issues don't just affect internal reporting, planning, forecasting and making business decisions. They affect the software and automation that drives these outcomes. As the old adage goes, rubbish in, rubbish out (well, that's the polite version anyway) and this has never been truer than with AI (Artificial Intelligence).

According to Wikipedia (2021), AI is intelligence demonstrated by machines, unlike the natural intelligence displayed by humans and animals, which involves consciousness and emotionality. The traditional problems (or goals) of AI research include reasoning, knowledge representation, planning, learning, natural language processing, perception and the ability to move and manipulate objects.

General intelligence is among AI's long-term goals. Approaches include statistical methods, computational intelligence and traditional symbolic AI. Many tools are used in AI, including versions of search and mathematical optimisation, artificial neural networks and methods based on statistics, probability and economics. The AI field draws upon computer science, information engineering, mathematics, psychology, linguistics, philosophy and many other fields.

What does this mean in a business context? According to *Harvard Business Review* (2018), there are three common types of AI being used in business: Process Automation, Cognitive Insight and Cognitive Engagement. In all forms, the AI is trying to simulate human intelligence and replace the human aspect of labour. In my world, this could be supplier normalisation and spend data classification; in another context it could be using it for analytics to make predictions on things like consumer behaviour, or even something like a chatbot. We've all been there, right? You get stuck in a loop where your question doesn't get answered and frustration kicks in.

There's also Robotic Process Automation (RPA), which is a form of automation but is intended to enhance and improve processes for humans, rather than ultimately replace them. For example, scanning/reading invoices from many different formats and adding them to the company's finance system. In this particular case, it's more efficient and accurate for RPA to do this task, as humans will undoubtedly make mistakes and work at a much slower pace.

While all these technologies absolutely have their place in the world and are doing some great things, particularly in the medical and science space amongst others, it can be more complex than this in business. The AI needs training data sets to learn from in order to learn and think like a human. This is particularly difficult in spend data classification because context is so often key when making a decision on how to classify something. AI needs lots of training sets. Lots and lots of training sets.

Let's go back to the IBM cleaning classification scenario. If this data had been used as a training set for spend data classification, every time that particular description and IBM in combination came up, it could be automatically classified as cleaning services. Now, imagine you are using this to update your data during a quarterly refresh. That £20k line of cleaning services could become £40k at the next refresh, or even higher. If that's not being checked, it could go even higher in future refreshes until it is flagged as an issue.

What does this mean? Firstly, the amount you are spending on cleaning is over-inflated. You could take the total figure of spend on cleaning and put out to tender a contract for a supplier to provide that amount of service over a specific time period, but as soon as the contract begins, it becomes apparent that there is not the amount of cleaning required that was in the contract. That's if you have an honest supplier who tells you that, or monitoring the contract otherwise, you are paying way over the odds for the service and you might never know.

The other issue is that your spend with IBM is understated. If you have a global data set, you might even be trying to negotiate a global contract. You could be getting a better global price for the technology you are buying, but you don't realise that because your data has not been classified correctly or been checked. Say the contract is fixed for three or five years, just think how much more money you could you be saving.

Another example would be DHL. If the AI is just classifying based on training data sets, it could become confused. A business like mine would be using DHL for courier and postal services, yet a large manufacturer or retailer would be using them for warehousing, supply chain and logistics. Without the context or knowledge of the situation, this could be incorrectly classified.

In my line of work, it is difficult to use any form of automation because I work across a range of different industries with a number of different taxonomies. If you are looking to buy an off-the-shelf automated solution, I would suggest this is unlikely to provide you with the quality and results you need. However, if you choose to develop something in-house that is specific to your business, you are likely to have greater success because all the training data being used will be similar and relevant. As long as the classification is correct, the AI output has a greater chance of being correct. But it still needs to be checked!

## How to ensure data accuracy

Firstly, to manage your expectations, don't expect that your data will be 100% accurate. If it is, it won't stay like that for long as people start to use and work with it. Cut and paste errors, accidental deletions and incorrect formulas can happen very easily within live data and they might not get picked up until much later, by which time it could be difficult to fix.

A more realistic approach is to aim for your data to be as accurate as possible. I've heard chief data officers (CDOs) talk about accurate data to them being 'fit for purpose'. What this means will be different for each company, and possibly each department within a company, depending on the type of data you are working with. For example, it would not be appropriate to have 'fit for purpose' data in accounting as that does have to be 100% accurate by law.

In procurement, as long as the data is as accurate as possible and the top 80-90% of spend is accurately classified, that would be acceptable to a number of procurement managers. If it is customer records/information, as long as certain fields are populated, that could be acceptable for a CDO.

I hate to break it to you, but there's no quick fix, magic button or special software out there that can magically fix your data. It requires hard work, patience and a commitment to better data accuracy. Yes, there are some software solutions that can help you manage and clean your data, but you will need a person to verify this and it only works on certain data, such as address and name verification and formatting - it is not going to help with the classification of spend data or normalisation.

## The human element

NEW DATA NEEDS TO BE SEEN BY A HUMAN FIRST TIME. As I've mentioned previously, context is so important in data. Whether it's procurement, financial, customer or supplier data, it needs to be reviewed by someone who is an expert in that specific area. If you are working with your data on a regular basis, it is much easier to spot when things don't look right if you are familiar with the data. It can be things such as layout, patterns in the data or even the numbers that flag up when something is wrong.

I also think it's really important to get the whole organisation involved, not just the IT or data departments. Whether it's someone in inventory who has to input the correct product information when setting up a new item, to a marketing assistant updating e-mail lists, it's vital everyone understands their roles and the consequences of what happens when they don't populate the data correctly or have inaccuracies.

Think back to the person setting up new products. They accidentally miss out a number from the product code they've set up or the description isn't accurate, or perhaps they input the incorrect product dimensions.

Either one of those situations could cause serious problems to the business.

In the first instance, if the description is incorrect, other people within the organisation will not be able to find that new product on a keyword search, which they might need to fulfil orders or purchase the new product. They may think the product has not been set up and so raise a request for it to be done. This could lead to a duplicate record and duplicate work. That's unnecessary time spent re-entering something that already exists and creates two records that might need to be merged, again spending unnecessary valuable time fixing and resolving the issue.

It's the same if the code is incorrect. What if the incorrect code is actually a different product? Or if it can't be found and so a request to set up a new item is raised. So much time that could be spent on the business in other important areas is being wasted. Think of all the time spent in conversations, trying to find the right person to speak to, figuring out where the problem is, chasing up people, possibly even speaking to customers to explain why something is delayed. It costs time and money and potentially causes reputational damage.

If you're supplying a customer with an item and the dimensions are incorrect it can incur significant costs. Deliveries are planned on how many items are on a pallet and how many pallets you can get on a specific type of truck. If this is automated and is worked out in a system, the first time this product is loaded onto a pallet/truck it won't be correct. This could mean deliveries are held up or even cancelled and that product then can't be shipped until the issue has been corrected. You could be charged by the logistics company for a failed collection, the customer could cancel the order . . . the list goes on.

If we don't tell the people inputting this information that this could be the consequence, how will they know? They might think it doesn't matter if they get something a bit wrong, that business will just carry on as usual.

It's the same for the marketing assistant. Due to data protection laws in many countries, it is vital that mailing lists are kept up to date and accurate, otherwise the company could have a huge fine imposed. When I set up my limited company, the letters started arriving from accountants and banks who all wanted me as their new client/customer. I received one letter with my first and middle name and someone else's surname. The business name was not mine either, but the mailing address was correct. The possibilities of how this happened include: not having the correct filters on and editing the data, a cut and paste error or a formula with inconsistencies. If this data is wrong, not only is it potentially illegal, but it also doesn't reflect well on you as a company.

The problem should have been picked up at a quality assurance (QA) stage, where the data should have been spot-checked to pick up any errors. This is not my specific area of expertise, but I'm sure there are many methods available out there that could prevent this from happening.

While a huge fine is not good, if you have duplicates it doesn't look good if your customer receives multiple e-mails. It's also financially inefficient if you are mailing these people multiple items that are the same. Think of all the wasted money or the items that could have been sent to new customers instead, not forgetting how it looks to the people you have mailed, which could be particularly damaging depending on what you do. In the example of my letter above, this was for an accountancy firm. How could I trust them with my financial data when they can't get my personal data right?

## How can you minimise errors?

It's really important to agree on common standards, terms and processes. This could be company-wide or within specific departments. I'm not talking about master data governance or data dictionaries here, as this can intimidate those who are not in the data profession. However, you do need a few standards, such as how to report 'litres' and in what format; what criteria is a must for setting up new customers/products; and how do you classify supplier X/Y/Z, etc. If you get the users of the data involved, it's more likely that they will adopt these processes and standards as they helped create them. Hopefully, that means time saved, stressful situations averted, avoidable costs prevented and a more efficiently run business.

Unfortunately though, that's not enough. You can't have accurate data and just expect it to stay like that. New data is constantly being created, so you have to maintain, manage and update it. From a procurement perspective, spend data isn't static. The business is constantly buying new things and that data has to be managed by normalising and classifying it so that you can get up-to-date visibility on what you're spending, with which company, and how much. This will help you monitor contract compliance, manage budgets, negotiate better rates with suppliers, manage the number of suppliers you have and make cost savings.

If you're using product data, it's more about making sure nothing has changed on the product, such as the dimensions or weight, or if the manufacturer's code has changed. It might seem like an obvious point to make, but these things can change without anyone realising and cause some of the issues previously discussed.

The same applies to master data. You might normalise or have a parent-child relationship with some of the suppliers, but companies can rebrand

and change their name or get bought by other companies, therefore it's not good enough to update your data once and leave it; you have to maintain and update it where necessary.

Keeping your data clean is just like good housekeeping – it needs to be checked and maintained on a regular basis. In the same way you give your carpets a regular once-over with the vacuum, regularly maintaining your data makes life easier in the long run. Remember, the more data you have, the more frequently you should check it.

## Spot-checking

This is important in all aspects of data because things can change. Someone could accidentally delete a record or supplier, losing with it all the historical information. Back-ups and security are an obvious solution, but think of the time and number of people involved in restoring the information and what if you don't know how long it's been like that?

There are also accidental cut and paste errors and these might not be so easy to spot. Yes, you can put in place some measures like restricted access, lock cells, etc., but that is particularly difficult to achieve in Excel and you don't always realise you've made an error. If you have filters on and try to cut and paste, it can end up overwriting some of the data that has been filtered out and you might not notice this for some time if you don't carry out regular maintenance and spot checks.

Then there's opinion. This is particularly prevalent in areas like spend data classification where, because it's so subjective, there can often be more than one right answer. Some people may take it upon themselves to amend the data to fit their beliefs and assumptions, causing incorrect or misleading information that could lead to bad business decisions.

This could also easily happen in product management as there may be more than one way to name a product. Whoever sets a product up on the system is instructed to do so in a particular way or in the way the manufacturer describes it, but someone in another department might disagree with this and change it to the name they are familiar with. For example, most of you will be familiar with Allen keys, those L-shaped, hexagon tools that are used to build furniture from a well known Swedish furniture retailer. They are also known as 'hex keys' and so someone might overwrite the product name based on their opinion, even if you have agreed standards and terminology in place. This could lead to product duplication and is another reason why it is so important to spot-check and maintain your data.

## How frequently should you check your data?

Let's go back to the carpet analogy. Leaving it for a week doesn't matter. It doesn't really matter if you leave it for a month (if you're okay with living with dirty carpets that is). However, if you leave that once clean carpet for too long, by the time you get out your vacuum cleaner, your carpet will be incredibly hard to clean, all the dirt will be mixed up and it could potentially be beyond saving.

Data is very much like that carpet. If you maintain it and spot-check regularly, it's far more manageable and easier to spot any incorrect information. If it's left too long, it could be such a big job to rectify that it ends up never getting done and the data gets progressively worse.

Data that's not maintained will slowly become unusable over time. Incorrect or conflicting information will build up. AI outputs become corrupted. Because you can't afford to use bad data, you end up spending significant time and money on fixing the problem. There are different levels of data quality services and you could end up paying a lot of money to fix the problem.

The amount of data you have will determine how often you should maintain it. I always suggest monthly or quarterly; anything more frequent becomes unproductive and the time/cost benefit rarely pays off. On the flip side, anything more than six-monthly and you will end up losing the integrity of the data and it most certainly will have lost its COAT (see page 17).

## Who should manage and maintain your data?

If you can, I would always recommend maintaining your data in-house. A side benefit of this is that they know the data better, they can tell far more quickly when something looks out of place and can correct it as soon as they see it. This skill only comes from working with data regularly. This works for me with the many files I have classified over the last decade. Within one day I can get a feel for the data, what it should look like, any patterns and what the spend values should be. If anything doesn't look right, I can spot it far more quickly in the following days because I've become familiar with it.

Can you just put tighter controls on your data and who has access to it to ensure its accuracy? No, and here's why I think it is a bad idea. Firstly, to have one or a few people managing the data is a mammoth task. They won't all be experts in every area of the data and some detail could get lost. It could also lead to a backlog in the data being updated, which in itself could cause further problems for areas such as reporting and decision making. Secondly, you might find that users of the data within the organisation start saving their own local copies of data/reports and you lose complete visibility on certain areas of the business unless you ask for a snapshot of their data. I see this as even more dangerous than having multiple users access the data. At least with multiple users you still have complete visibility of what's going on in your organisation. (Okay, well not 100% - we all know people like to save their own special files locally, but it will help minimise the issue.)

It's about empowering people to own and manage the data they work with and to understand the consequences of dirty data. Each business will have its own consequences, but it's important to know what these are and to communicate them to the people working with the data.

Sadly, it's also not that easy. Not everyone who works with data or inputs it is skilled or experienced in this area and there might be an assumption that they are. It can be intimidating for a lot of people and that's often why things don't get done or are incorrect. I've created a way to address this as I want all data users to be comfortable working with and managing data. If you have learned anything from me in this book so far, you will know that I like to have fun and make data fun, so make sure your data has its COAT on!

## Get your COAT

You read it correctly, give your data a COAT. Think of it like this; you wouldn't go out in freezing temperatures without the appropriate coat and you shouldn't work with data or make business decisions without the same level of protection - and that protection is *accurate data*.

### C is for consistent

Generally, data is used by many people or teams, which can lead to multiple classifications of one product or service. For example, quite often consultants will list out their charges on an invoice. Each line is reported, but some of the charges related to their consultancy services is travel. Some people might classify it in this instance as Professional Services and another person might classify it as Travel, so agree some common standards to ensure this type of spend is classified in the same way.

It could even be those units of measure again. Is everyone using the same terminology? One person may use 'litre', another 'ltr' and another 'l' - but these should all be one consistent format. This means everything can be reported accurately, you get a true picture of what's going on and better business decisions can be made.

## O is for organised

Data is only useful if it's organised. Think of a messy closet: you're looking for your favourite top but can't find it as everything has been thrown in there. If you had organised it properly, grouping similar types of clothing together (even by colour if you really want), you'd be able to find it quickly and easily and it would have less chance of being creased.

Much like your closet, you can organise your data in different ways depending on what you want to get out of it and to help produce different reports and analytics. You may want to organise and split data by employees, teams, departments, functions or internal categories, as well as periods such as months and quarters. So, for example, when you need the information on the accounts that Dave in Finance is working on or the sales team's performance for the quarter, you can pull that information quickly.

## A is for accurate

This can mean different things to different organisations, but at its most basic level, accurate data is correct data. This could mean no duplicate information; correct invoice descriptions; correct classifications; no missing product codes; standard units of measure (e.g. ltr, l, litres); no currency issues; correctly spelt suppliers; fully classified data; or the right data in the right columns.

Accurate data allows for greater visibility across your business and better decisions, as well as time and cost savings and increased profits.

## T is for trustworthy

This is critical. Business decisions around jobs, staffing, budgets, cost savings and more are all based on data. Data is used by everyone from the bottom to the top of an organisation. You have to be able to trust that what you're looking at is the right information and you need it to be accurate in order for your teams to use the data in their daily jobs.

If you or your team don't trust the data, the fancy new software you've just spent tens of thousands of pounds installing (or the new AI you've developed) might not produce the right results because it's learning from dirty data.

Just like with coats, there are many different levels of data services out there. If you buy a cheap jacket, it might not be waterproof or protect you from the elements, it won't last much longer than one season and you'll need to buy another the next time winter comes around again. It's the same with data – if you don't invest in good quality service, whether internally or externally, you will end up paying twice as much, if not more, in the long run to fix the earlier mistakes. You don't want to be left out in the cold!

I can frequently be heard saying, 'Like a good coat, data is an investment – not a cost'. By making sure your data has its COAT on, you are saving time, money and avoiding future problems. Like any coat, it does of course need to be maintained. You need to continually ensure your data is consistent, organised, accurate and trustworthy to get the most out of it.

## General Data Protection Regulation (GDPR)

Unfortunately, there's no avoiding it: let's talk about the regulations around personal data. While a lot of what I will be talking about in this book is financial data, Chapter 5 demonstrates how to clean personal data, so it's important to cover this off.

Where you are based will determine how you are governed. If you live in the European Union (EU) or the European Economic Area (EEA) (the EU, plus Iceland, Lichtenstein and Norway), you are subject to the laws of GDPR. However, even if you are based outside of the EU, such as the United States of America (USA), but have offices in the EU and process data of EU subjects, you still need to comply.

It's a complete minefield and I am going to try my best to navigate you through these swampy GDPR waters. There's going to be lots of formal style sentences, which really aren't my thing, but when it comes to GDPR, you really can't escape it.

### What is GDPR?

GDPR is the General Data Protection Regulation and is a set of legislation laid out by the European Union (EU) on dealing with personal data. It applies to anyone doing business in or with another organisation based in the EU. These rules came into force on 25 May 2018 and although it's unlikely you'll need to know them in great depth (thank goodness), it's always sensible for anyone who handles data to be familiar with the regulations surrounding the data they're working with.

GDPR has two purposes: (1) to standardise data protection law across the EU single market; and (2) to give people greater control over how their personal information is used and processed. Non-compliance comes with heavy penalties. Organisations that fail to comply could be liable for fines of up to £17 million pounds or 4% of their turnover, whichever is greater. It's a serious business.

### Does GDPR apply in the UK?

How does GDPR affect the UK post-Brexit? According to the Information Commissioner's Office (ICO):

> The key principles, rights and obligations remain the same. However, there are implications for the rules on transfers of personal data between the UK and the EEA.
>     The UK GDPR also applies to controllers and processors based outside the UK if their processing activities relate to:
>
> * offering goods or services to individuals in the UK; or
> * monitoring the behaviour of individuals taking place in the UK.
>
> There are also implications for UK controllers who have an establishment in the EEA, have customers in the EEA, or monitor individuals in the EEA. The EU GDPR still applies to this processing, but the way you interact with European data protection authorities has changed.
>     https://ico.org.uk/for-organisations/dp-at-the-end-of-the-transition-period/
>     data-protection-now-the-transition-period-has-ended/the-gdpr/

Did you get that? No, me neither to be honest. I wish they would just say in simple terms what you can and can't do.

### What type of privacy does GDPR cover?

* Basic identity information such as name, address and ID numbers
* Web data such as location, IP address, cookie data and Radio Frequency ID (RFID) tags
* Health and genetic data
* Biometric data
* Racial or ethnic data
* Political opinions
* Sexual orientation.

### What rights do people have under GDPR?

The GDPR expands the rights of individuals (referred to in the legislation as 'data subjects') over the use of their data compared with the previous Data Protection Act 1998. Those rights include:

* the right to be informed
* the right of access to information without charge and within one month of their request

- the right to object to processing likely to cause or causing damage or distress
- the right to prevent processing for direct marketing
- the right to object to decisions being taken by automated means, including profiling
- the right to have inaccurate data rectified
- the right to restrict processing
- in certain situations, the right to have data deleted (commonly referred to as 'the right to be forgotten')
- the right of data portability, where they can request, and reuse, data held and instruct its transfer from one data controller to another, i.e. for changing supplier.

### How does this affect me/my company?

GDPR defines several roles that are required for the responsibility of ensuring compliance: the data controller, the data processor and the data protection officer (DPO). It's the job of the data controller to decide how personal data is processed and the purposes for which it is processed. The controller is also responsible for making sure that people like outside contractors comply. The data processors could be internal groups that maintain and process personal data records, but they could also be any outsourcing firm that performs all or part of those activities. If you're a small business like me, then you could be both.

Under the legislation, a 'data processor' is any entity that processes personal data on behalf of the 'data controller'. The difference between controllers and processors is that processors have no control over what data is collected and what it is used for; they merely facilitate the collection of data and/or use it for set purposes decided by the controller.

Previous legislation didn't apply to data processors, but now under the GDPR it means the ICO will be able to take enforcement action against data processors, including issuing fines. They can also be held liable for compensation to data subjects for failure to comply with the GDPR and/or process the personal data as instructed by the controller. This is why it's really important to make sure you don't have dirty personal data. It's not someone else's problem, it's all of our responsibility.

### How do I stay compliant?

This can all sound quite scary, but staying compliant isn't too complicated if you take some simple steps:

- only act on your documented instructions
- don't contract a sub-processor without prior approval
- delete or return all personal data at the end of the contract.

Those are the basics of GDPR. If you are unsure, or have any questions, I would suggest using the ICO website if you're in the UK (https://ico.org.uk), or the European Commission website if you're in Europe (https://ec.europa.eu/info/law/law-topic/data-protection_en).

Your organisation might also require you to carry out risk assessments or audits to ensure your compliance with GDPR. If you can demonstrate high-security standards and an understanding of your obligations under the terms of your contract, you should have nothing to worry about. However, data protection is serious business and it's always worth taking a bit of extra time to ensure you fully understand your obligations.

### What if I don't live in the EU, EEA or the UK?

You will have local laws governing the use of personal data. I would not even attempt to list them all here, so please check locally for guidance if you live elsewhere. Regardless of the laws you fall under, please, always try and keep that data clean!

I could go into the scare stories of how much large companies have been fined, but quite frankly I'm not sure it's working. According to DLA Piper's research (2021), there's a 19% increase in breach notifications of GDPR, resulting in EUR272.5 million of fines in 2020. Some might argue this is because the regulators are getting tougher, and that might be true, but the fact still remains that these companies were misusing personal data and had inaccurate information. The regulations changed in 2018 so there's been plenty of time to address these issues.

The bigger issue is changing the attitude and culture towards data quality and accuracy. I hope this book can be used as a tool to help change that mindset. If all these companies are going to get fined is a maximum of 4% of their turnover, I think we could see the number of fines increasing without any change in attitude or behaviour.

### How to maintain and spot-check your data

Earlier in this chapter, we discussed how the more regularly you check your data, the easier your job will become. By regularly I don't necessarily mean weekly, or even monthly, but quarterly will help massively. Data changes so regular maintenance and spot-checking is essential. It is constantly being used and sometimes abused by others. Mistakes happen, someone might cut and paste or there could be an accidental deletion of some important information. It happens all the time.

While no one likes to think about it, fraud can happen too. If you have multiple people checking and maintaining the data, this can be a way to help minimise the issue. The more frequently you check or work with your data, the easier it is to spot when things don't look quite right as you are more familiar with its patterns, structure and flow. Even things like high values against certain suppliers will stand out if you are familiar with their typical spend, or if you're working with products, it could be that the quantities don't look right.

Regularly checking your data also stops the manifestation of issues, like the IBM cleaning classification, for example. This in turn will save you or your organisation time and money, and who doesn't want that?

I'm going to show you how to do this in Excel, which means if you have a large volume of data it might not like it. If that's the case, try and break the data down into smaller chunks, such as division of the company, by year, by quarter, or even by the supplier if there are a significant number of rows.

In my examples, I will be using some spend data where the suppliers have already been normalised (which I'll cover in detail in Chapter 2). Using your data, create a pivot table. If you only have partially classified data, it's up to you whether you want to include this in your checks or not. If you don't want to, you can untick the blanks in the normalised name column. If you want to do a quick check of suppliers and classifications, you can choose to look at the normalised name and classifications without the description.

As you can see (Figure 1.1 on the next page), the layout is not ideal and we want to make it as easy as possible to find any classification errors, so under the Design tab, go to Report Layout and select Show in Tabular Form (Figure 1.2, page 25).

This is starting to look much better, but as you can see (Figure 1.3, page 26), when it reformats into a table, you can now see totals, which are unnecessary and distracting. You can remove these by going to Subtotals and Grand totals in the Design tab (Figure 1.4, page 27).

Now you have data in an appropriate format for the next step, which is spot-checking the classified data. If you are doing it by supplier level only, there are two ways you can check the data. The first is to scroll down and look at the multiple classifications against a supplier. If you regularly check your data, you'll become familiar with the suppliers or products or even the codes, which will make this exercise easier.

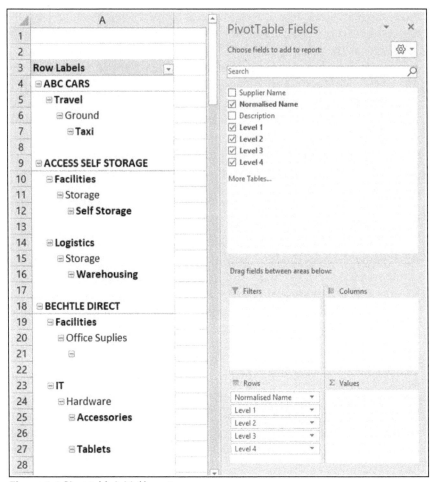

**Figure 1.1** *Pivot table initial layout*

Immediately, I can tell that with Access Self Storage (Figure 1.5, page 28) there is an incorrect classification. Firstly, because this supplier comes up a lot in the data I classify and I know it should only have one classification and that should be self storage. Secondly, if you didn't have my knowledge, the name of the company should give away what the classification should be. Finally, the Logistics and Warehousing classifications tell me that this is the wrong category for this supplier.

Don't be tricked into thinking that just because the first level is correct, the *whole* classification is correct. While the most important thing to do is get your Level 1 right, it's just as important to get your Level 2 correct (and Levels 3, 4 and beyond if you can). Remember, you have to make sure that data has its COAT on and is consistent, organised, accurate and trustworthy.

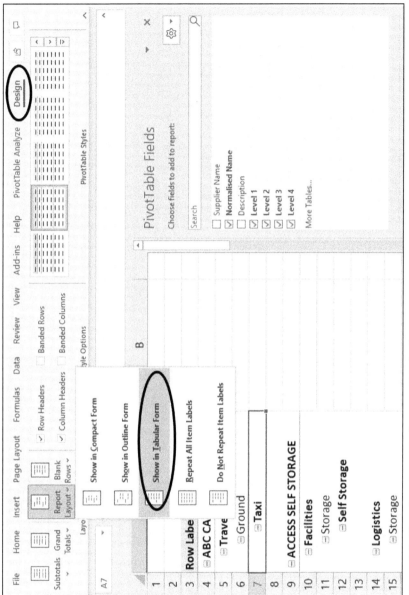

**Figure 1.2** *Changing pivot table format to Tabular Form*

Getting those levels right could be the difference between the data being classified as cleaning services or property rent if it sits under Facilities at Level 1. These are the category levels that will be looked at with most scrutiny by senior managers in meetings, mainly via visualisations such as charts, which could make the error stand out even more and lead to them questioning the trustworthiness of the whole data set.

| Normalised Name | Level 1 | Level 2 | Level 3 | Level 4 |
|---|---|---|---|---|
| ⊟ **ABC CARS** | ⊟ **Travel** | ⊟ Ground | ⊟ **Taxi** | |
| | | | Taxi Total | |
| | | Ground Total | | |
| | Travel Total | | | |
| ABC CARS Total | | | | |
| ⊟ **ACCESS SELF STORAGE** | ⊟ **Facilities** | ⊟ Storage | ⊟ **Self Storage** | |
| | | | Self Storage Total | |
| | | Storage Total | | |
| | Facilities Total | | | |
| | ⊟ **Logistics** | ⊟ Storage | ⊟ **Warehousing** | |
| | | | Warehousing Total | |
| | | Storage Total | | |
| | Logistics Total | | | |
| ACCESS SELF STORAGE Total | | | | |
| ⊟ **BECHTLE DIRECT** | ⊟ **Facilities** | ⊟ Office Suplies | ⊟ | |
| | | | Total | |
| | | Office Suplies Total | | |
| | Facilities Total | | | |
| | ⊟ **IT** | ⊟ Hardware | ⊟ **Accessories** | |
| | | | Accessories Total | |
| | | | ⊟ **Tablets** | |
| | | | Tablets Total | |
| | | Hardware Total | | |
| | IT Total | | | |

**Figure 1.3** *Updated pivot table layout*

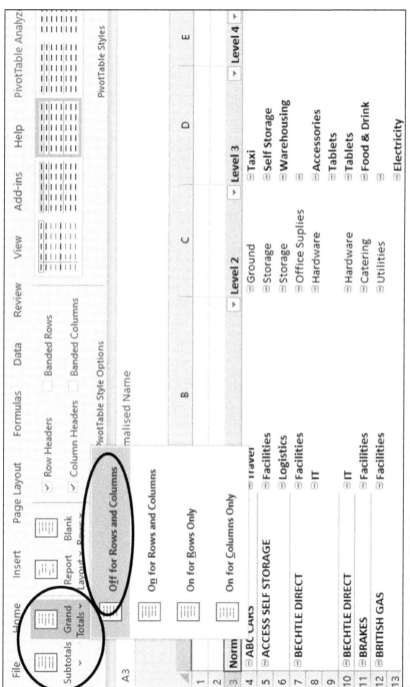

**Figure 1.4** *Removing Grand Totals from a pivot table*

| Normalised Name | Level 1 | Level 2 | Level 3 | Level 4 |
|---|---|---|---|---|
| ABC CARS | Travel | Ground | Taxi | |
| ACCESS SELF STORAGE | Facilities | Storage | Self Storage | |
| | Logistics | Storage | Warehousing | |
| BECHTLE DIRECT | Facilities | Office Suplies | | |
| | IT | Hardware | Accessories | |
| | | | Tablets | |
| BECHTLE DIRECT | IT | Hardware | Tablets | |
| BRAKES | Facilities | Catering | Food & Drink | |
| BRITISH GAS | Facilities | Utilities | Electricity | |
| DELL | Facilities | Post & Courier | Courier | |
| | IT | Hardware | Computers | |
| | | | Peripherals | |
| | | | Servers | |
| | | IT Services | | |
| | | Software | | |
| DELOITTE | Professional Services | Financial Services | Audit | |

**Figure 1.5**  *Checking for classification errors in the pivot table*

Let's make sure that doesn't happen! You can check it the way I've just described, as well as the alternative, if you want to be extra thorough and you are familiar with your suppliers and the products or services they provide. You can also filter by each category at Level 1, for example, if you see ABC Taxis in a Facilities category, then you know this is wrong as it should be in Travel. It might be more subtle than that, but if you know your data, you'll be able to spot it. This experience comes with regular spot-checking and maintenance.

If you have a lot of changes to make, you don't want to be flipping between screens or tabs to make the changes. It's cumbersome and might put people off doing the job properly. I'm all about working efficiently, so I have a solution for you.

In the view tab, select New Window (Figure 1.6 on the next page). At this point it might feel like nothing has happened, but you've created an identical view of the spreadsheet you have open. The only giveaway that there's another is, whatever the file is called, it will be the same name but with a number 2 at the end. In my example, I have my classified file open and the second version is called classified 2.

Next, you'll need to go back to the View tab and this time click on Arrange All (Figure 1.7, page 31). A pop-up box will appear and you have the choice of how you'd like to view the sheets. In this instance, I'd like a Vertical view, but if you were working with a spreadsheet with fewer rows but lots of columns, you might want the Horizontal view.

Your view should look like this (Figure 1.8, page 32). Initially, it will be a mirror image of the same tab in the spreadsheet, so change one of them to the tab with the raw data. This means you can now search in the pivot tab and then immediately correct it in the raw data tab. Don't forget to click the Refresh All button in the Data tab on the ribbon at the top; this will update the data in your pivot tab and will make sure you don't end up going over the same dirty data. Again, it's all about working efficiently.

The checking by supplier name method should pick up quickly anything that doesn't look right. But what if you're in an industry like manufacturing, where every nut, bolt, screw and tool needs to be tracked? Searching by supplier name just won't cut it, so if you're looking for a more in-depth check of your data, create a pivot as before, but this time include the description.

You might be thinking that you could just search the raw data. That would be fine, but if you have a large number of rows, you'll have multiple versions of the same description. By using a pivot, this will aggregate to a unique combination of supplier and description, reducing the number of rows, and will make the spot-checking process much easier.

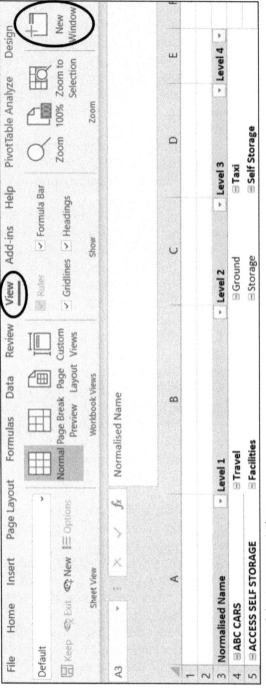

**Figure 1.6** *Selecting a new window*

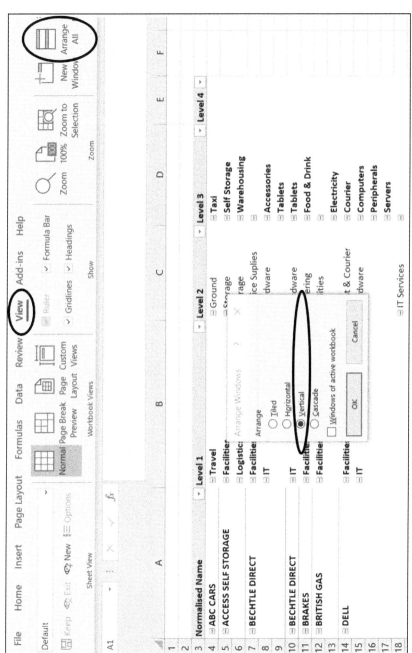

**Figure 1.7** How to Arrange All views vertically

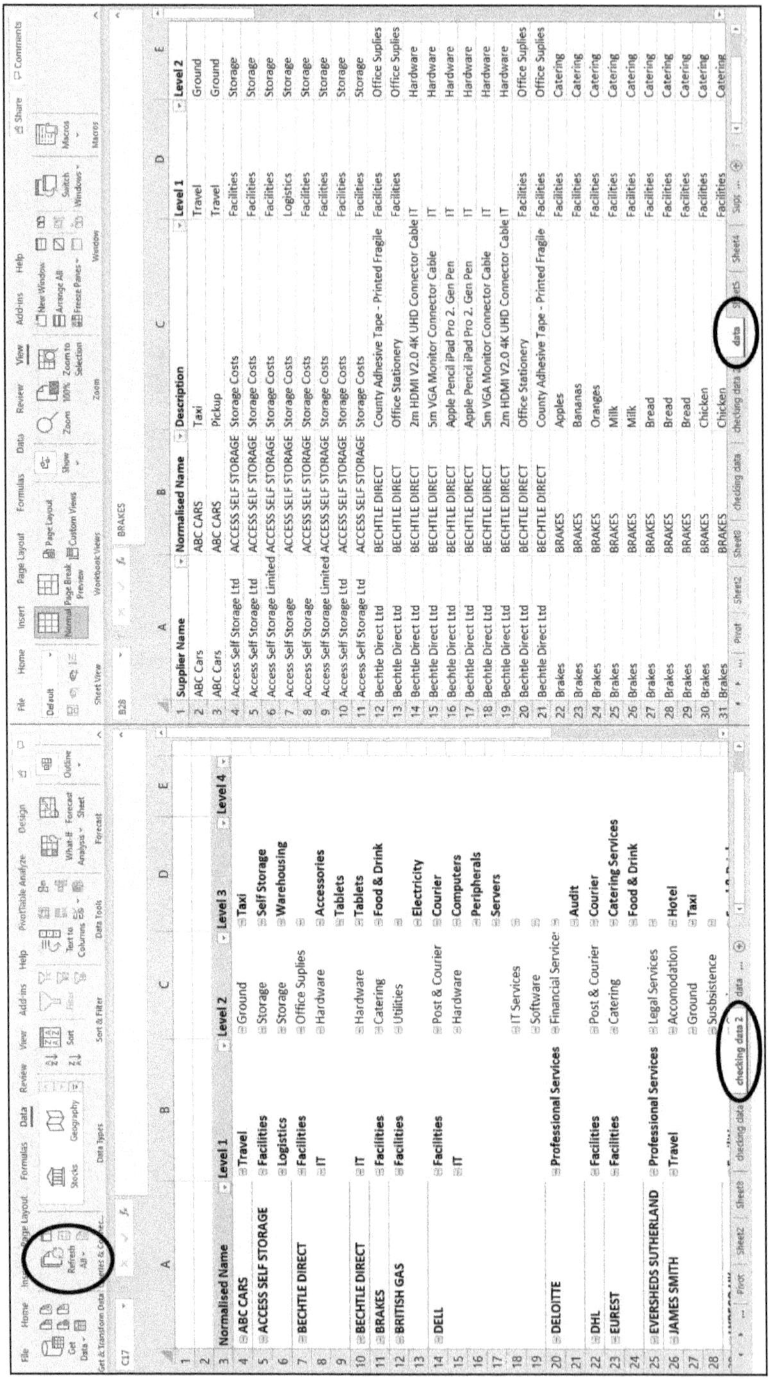

**Figure 1.8** *Views arranged vertically*

As with the supplier name spot check, create the pivot, select Tabular Form and remove the Subtotals. You'll find that the pivot table might leave blank spaces where a name or description appears more than once (Figure 1.9). If you're happy with that, you can spot-check in this format. However, if you think that might be difficult, you can automatically fill in the empty rows by selecting Repeat All Item Labels in the Design tab (Figure 1.10 on the next page).

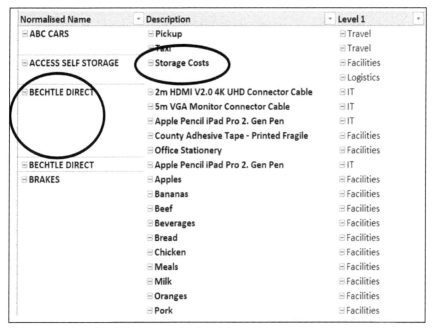

| Normalised Name | Description | Level 1 |
|---|---|---|
| ABC CARS | Pickup | Travel |
| | Taxi | Travel |
| ACCESS SELF STORAGE | Storage Costs | Facilities |
| | | Logistics |
| BECHTLE DIRECT | 2m HDMI V2.0 4K UHD Connector Cable | IT |
| | 5m VGA Monitor Connector Cable | IT |
| | Apple Pencil iPad Pro 2. Gen Pen | IT |
| | County Adhesive Tape - Printed Fragile | Facilities |
| | Office Stationery | Facilities |
| BECHTLE DIRECT | Apple Pencil iPad Pro 2. Gen Pen | IT |
| BRAKES | Apples | Facilities |
| | Bananas | Facilities |
| | Beef | Facilities |
| | Beverages | Facilities |
| | Bread | Facilities |
| | Chicken | Facilities |
| | Meals | Facilities |
| | Milk | Facilities |
| | Oranges | Facilities |
| | Pork | Facilities |

**Figure 1.9** *Example of blank spaces in pivot table*

As you can see (Figure 1.11, page 35), visually it's easier to follow all the supplier names and the descriptions. In the example below, having storage costs listed twice flags that there is more than one classification. For me, that stands out more than having just the unique names and descriptions. My not-so-secret tip to checking classified data is to look for patterns and trends within the data.

From here you can start to perform keyword searches, such as nuts, bolts, screws, etc. (I'll cover this in greater detail in Chapter 4 – Spend Data Classification.) I'd recommend using the same process of adding in the extra window outlined above so you can view the pivot tab and the raw data tab at the same time, correcting any errors as you find them. It's all about working smarter and more efficiently.

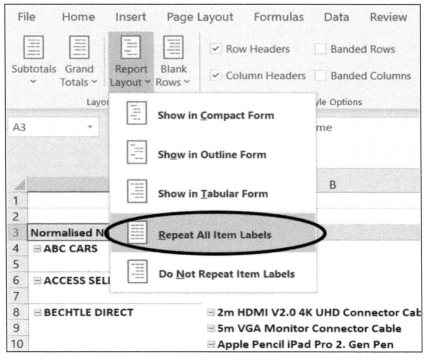

**Figure 1.10** *How to Repeat All Item Labels in pivot*

## Conclusion

That concludes this chapter. I hope that you've enjoyed reading about dirty data, understanding that it comes in many forms, such as misspelt names, incorrect or misleading descriptions, missing or incorrect codes, no standard formatting or units of measure, currency issues, incorrect or partially classified spend data and, of course, our old friend, the duplicate. There will be more in your own organisation and the important thing is to be aware of what they are so you can deal with them. We've also covered the consequences if you don't!

This chapter has also helped you understand the importance of why data needs to be cleansed. I've given you the spot-checking tips to enable you to do this, so why not try it on your own data as soon as you can, even just a small sample. You might be horrified, or at least surprised (unless you work with your data regularly, then it will come as no surprise), but remember this is a good thing as it means you are on the right path to improving your data and keeping it that way with regular maintenance.

I hope you've embraced COAT. Having consistent, organised, accurate and trustworthy data is so key and it's a way that anyone in your

| Normalised Name | Description | Level 1 | Level 2 | Level 3 | Level 4 |
|---|---|---|---|---|---|
| ABC CARS | Pickup | Travel | Ground | Taxi | |
| ABC CARS | Taxi | Travel | Ground | Taxi | |
| ACCESS SELF STORAGE | Storage Costs | Facilities | Storage | Self Storage | |
| ACCESS SELF STORAGE | Storage Costs | Logistics | Storage | Warehousing | |
| BECHTLE DIRECT | 2m HDMI V2.0 4K UHD Connector Cable | IT | Hardware | Accessories | |
| BECHTLE DIRECT | 5m VGA Monitor Connector Cable | IT | Hardware | Accessories | |
| BECHTLE DIRECT | Apple Pencil iPad Pro 2. Gen Pen | IT | Hardware | Tablets | |
| BECHTLE DIRECT | County Adhesive Tape - Printed Fragile | Facilities | Office Suplies | | |
| BECHTLE DIRECT | Office Stationery | Facilities | Office Suplies | | |
| BECHTLE DIRECT | Apple Pencil iPad Pro 2. Gen Pen | IT | Hardware | Tablets | |
| BRAKES | Apples | Facilities | Catering | Food & Drink | |
| BRAKES | Bananas | Facilities | Catering | Food & Drink | |
| BRAKES | Beef | Facilities | Catering | Food & Drink | |
| BRAKES | Beverages | Facilities | Catering | Food & Drink | |
| BRAKES | Bread | Facilities | Catering | Food & Drink | |
| BRAKES | Chicken | Facilities | Catering | Food & Drink | |
| BRAKES | Meals | Facilities | Catering | Food & Drink | |
| BRAKES | Milk | Facilities | Catering | Food & Drink | |
| BRAKES | Oranges | Facilities | Catering | Food & Drink | |
| BRAKES | Pork | Facilities | Catering | Food & Drink | |

**Figure 1.11** *Pivot table with All Item Labels repeated*

organisation can get involved and understand the importance of data, but in an engaging way. If you don't quite remember the acronym yet, that's okay, as I will be dropping lots more hints about it as you progress through the chapters.

# 2 Supplier Normalisation

## What is supplier normalisation?

Let's start with why I'm referring to 'supplier normalisation' and not 'vendor normalisation'. I work with companies all over the world and I see the use of 'supplier' a lot in the UK and Europe, but 'vendor' occurs more frequently in the US. In my day to day, I alternate between supplier and vendor and use them interchangeably.

I created a poll on LinkedIn and asked my network what their preferred terminology is. I had no idea that it would cause such a debate! 1,184 people voted, over 200 commented and the final result was: 65% voted 'supplier' and 35% voted 'vendor'. I had some great comments for justification of each, including:

'I say vendor, but I believe supplier is correct, but "partner" is where we should strive to be.'

'Worth thinking about "third-party" too which is increasingly the terminology in Financial Services.'

'I use vendor because that's what I started with academically and how it's been referred to in my last three jobs.'

'Both supply goods and/or services. Vendors: B2C and B2B relationships. Suppliers: only B2B relationships.'

'I just had this conversation with a colleague . . . from my perspective it's most definitely "supplier". I haven't used the term "vendor" since the 90s.'

'Vendors are the people who sell hot dogs at a baseball game.'

'Supplier for sure. Vendor sounds non-important.'

'I had a supplier say to me one time, "We are not a vending machine". It stuck with me. I use the words interchangeably, sometimes it depends on the audience, but I think supplier sounds more professional.'

As you can see, it's not clear cut and both terms are widely accepted. For the purpose of this book, I will use supplier, which will also encompass anything vendor related.

Supplier normalisation can also be referred to as 'standardisation'. Normalisation is giving your existing suppliers a common name or grouping so that you can see how much you are truly spending with them or selling to them. When you are doing this for the first time, I would always recommend adding a new column to your spreadsheet. I would not recommend overwriting your existing suppliers as you may need this information in the future, and it will definitely help for classification, which I'll cover in Chapter 4.

Surely companies must know how much they are spending with, selling to or using their suppliers already? You would think so, but there are a number of reasons why you might find multiple versions of the same supplier in a database. One reason is that you have a global presence and each country has named their supplier as it is known in that locality. Quite often there are suffixes attached to companies such as Inc, Ltd, Limited, etc., that cause multiple versions of the same supplier. You could also have independent divisions of one company that all have their own naming conventions. When you add in typos and incorrect spellings you can see how easily duplicate accounts are created.

Another reason for inaccurate data could be acquisitions. When a company is bought and the data is integrated into the existing database, it can cause all sorts of problems and discrepancies, not least multiple variations of the same supplier. This leads into multiple source systems and is why there can be a lot of inconsistency.

Common suppliers where you might find multiple versions include:

**Table 2.1** *Common supplier names*

| 1 & 1 TELECOM GMBH | 1UND1 IONOS | 1&1 IONOS | 1&1 Internet | IONOS |
|---|---|---|---|---|
| Automatic Data Processing | A.D.P. | ADP Inc | ADP Ltd | ADP Limited |
| Dell Corporation | Dell Marketing | Dell Software | Dell Ltd | Dell Limited |
| IBM SP Z O O | IBM Limited | IBM Inc | IBM Ltd | I.B.M. |
| PriceWaterhouse Coopers | Price Waterhouse Coopers | PWC Inc | PWC Ltd | P.W.C. |

## Why does normalisation matter?

Ultimately, you could be making bad business decisions if you don't have all the correct information. If you are in procurement, you might have local arrangements with the supplier and the price you pay for the same item could vary hugely across regions, allowing the opportunity to negotiate a better global pricing agreement.

Likewise, to look at customer sales globally, you want to make sure you have the right information. You might think you are selling X amount to Customer A, but in fact, with normalisation, you could find it's a lot more than that. This could then affect rebates, commission, sales forecasts, marketing plans and production planning. Potentially, it has a huge knock-on effect.

With that knowledge, are you treating that customer fairly with the appropriate discounts and customer service? Can you afford to lose this customer or is there an opportunity to upsell to them? You can't make any of these decisions without the right information.

Again, for procurement, there could be a target to rationalise the number of suppliers you have agreements with. Supplier normalisation is an exceptionally efficient way of doing this – it's like eating chocolate without the calories! Referring back to a great example I mentioned in Chapter 1, a client of mine had 41,000 suppliers when I received their data. After normalisation this was reduced to 34,900. Just imagine – over 6,000 versions of the same supplier that could be immediately rationalised without any of the paperwork or effort to close accounts down. This process took me around five days to complete using my proprietary methodology and some off-the-shelf software. It can also be done in Excel, which I will show you later.

There are other hidden costs to having multiple versions of the same supplier or customer. A large one is invoice processing time. How much time are your colleagues spending on raising or processing multiple invoices for the same supplier or customer that could be condensed into one and processed in a much shorter time? This could also have a knock-on effect on things like time to pay, number of payment runs required and time saved reconciling accounts, freeing up your team to work more efficiently on other tasks.

## What about company parent/child relationships?

Some companies like to normalise their suppliers based on financial or corporate structures. An example would be IHG, the parent company of Holiday Inn and Intercontinental. In this example, it would be fine to normalise to IHG because it is all travel-related spend and so is easy to classify against that one supplier. Plus, you might be able to negotiate at that level on travel spend across all their brands.

However, there are other instances where it gets trickier. ABF (Associated British Foods) is a great example; their brands include Primark (clothing), Twinings (tea), AB Agri (animal nutrition) and British Sugar (food). Immediately, your spend could be sitting across multiple categories (not just travel-related spend as with IHG), which might not give a true picture of spend with that 'supplier'. I put that in inverted commas because in most cases you would probably not be negotiating with them as a parent company; it would be with each brand or sub-division individually and there would be no influence at the parent company.

That is why I normalise with the company names; it helps me classify and check classified data more effectively if I also have the original company name.

The only reason I would completely change the normalised name is if the company changes its name. For example, I have been classifying with Neopost as a supplier for years. It's instantly recognisable as a post/franking machine supplier, but they have recently changed their name to Quadient. In this instance, I would change the normalised name, otherwise the spend might sit across two different supplier names when in reality it's only one. However, I wouldn't interfere with the original supplier name – that should remain unchanged.

## Charts and visualisations

Normalisation can make a big impact on charts and visualisations.

Here is a great example (Figure 2.1 opposite) of where normalisation can make visualisations more powerful. Most decision makers will not be spending their time looking through spreadsheets and will want a top-level view of what's going on in the business.

If you want actionable, impactful visualisations, you need your data to have its COAT on. Normalisation is a great way to aid this process.

If you look at the chart at the top, it looks like there are a number of suppliers, none of which are spending over £80k. It gives your business *a* picture, but not necessarily the *right* picture. If decisions are made based on the chart at the top, a supplier rationalisation project might be implemented and time wasted looking at suppliers that don't need to be rationalised. Perhaps you or a colleague use this chart to go into a negotiation and your numbers don't match that of your suppliers because you're missing information. You'll not only lose some bargaining power, you may also lose credibility.

If you normalise your suppliers, you get the chart at the bottom, which is easy to read, contains accurate figures and gives the business the ability to make better decisions. You can confidently challenge your supplier's figures if you know your own sums are accurate and you might even save more for your organisation. That makes *you* look good, raises *your* profile in your own company and gives *you* credibility.

## Un-normalised suppliers

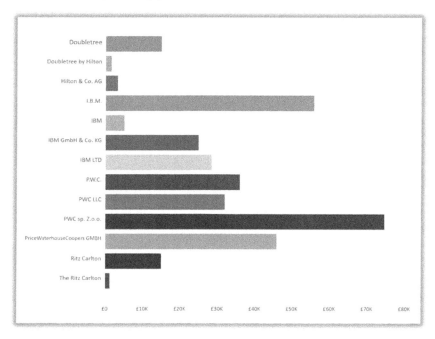

## Normalised suppliers

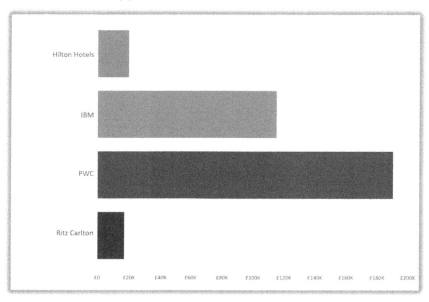

**Figure 2.1** *Normalised versus Un-normalised suppliers*

## Normalisation best practice and rules

As mentioned earlier in the chapter, the most important thing is to never overwrite the existing data. Create a new column called Normalised Supplier/Vendor (whatever works best for you) and work in this. That way you can always refer back to the original column if something goes wrong. I'd also recommend hiding any columns you don't need while doing this exercise, as they'll only be a distraction while normalising.

In that Normalised Supplier column (Figure 2.2), use the UPPER formula (Figures 2.2 and 2.3 opposite) to make sure all the suppliers are in upper case. It's important at this stage to remember to copy and paste with special values (Figure 2.4, page 44). If you don't, it can cause problems, not just in this situation but when using any formula.

If you try to edit the data in the cell, you should be reminded that it's a formula, but it's good practice to change to values straight away in case you lose any of the work you have done.

Why use upper case? The reason for doing this is that when you are scrolling through hundreds, if not thousands, of suppliers, it's hard to spot similar names, so having everything in upper case makes the process that little bit easier, faster and more effective. I have tried doing this in lower case, but it doesn't have the same effectiveness and you are more likely to overlook duplicates or near-duplicates if you have it in lower, proper or sentence case.

Next is my favourite part – the tidying up. I know that some people really hate this, but I LOVE it. There's something very satisfying about taking messy supplier data and turning it into useful, useable data for businesses.

It's not easy, but it is very rewarding. There are parts of this process that could be semi-automated with code, but because of the nature of the words and letters that are being removed, you have to be very careful not to remove sections of the supplier name that are there legitimately.

## The risky list

The common words and letters that you should be particularly cautious about, also known as the risky list, are:

| Table 2.2 *Words and letters on the risky list* | | |
|---|---|---|
| INC | S.A. | S.L. |
| CO | S.A | S.L |
| LIMITED | SA | SL |
| LTD | SAS | LLC |

| | A | B |
|---|---|---|
| | Supplier Name | Normalised Supplier |
| | "APENA KAFAYAT O." | =upper(A2) |
| | "BHASKAR MARKETING CO.," | |
| | "BJM" SP. Z O.O. | |
| | "Crimson Hexagon, Inc" | |
| | "EDUCA, CREA COMUNICA AC" | |
| | "GRILL PLUS" S.C. DARIUSZ WĄSAK, EWELINA TABOR-WĄSAK | |
| | "IDEAŁ" P. GROMEK, P. MUSZYŃSKI, S. MUSZYŃSKI SP. J. | |
| | "MIKOMAX SPÓŁKA Z OGRANICZONĄ ODPOWIEDZIALNOŚCIĄ" SPÓŁKA KOMANDYTOWA | |

**Figure 2.2**  *Using the UPPER formula*

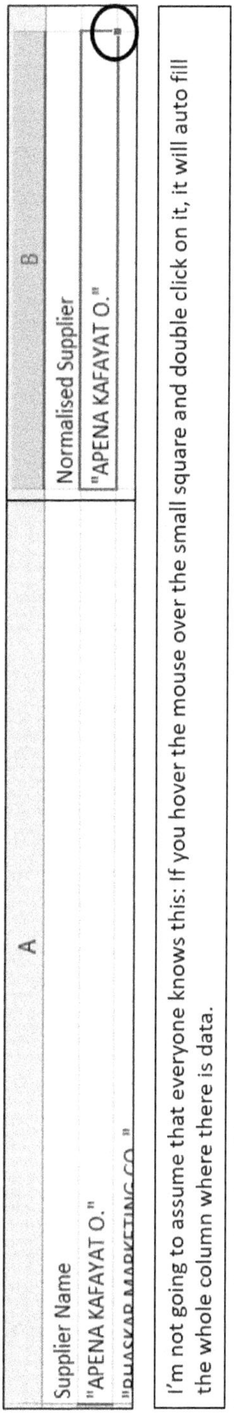

| | A | B |
|---|---|---|
| | Supplier Name | Normalised Supplier |
| | "APENA KAFAYAT O." | "APENA KAFAYAT O." |
| | "BHASKAR MARKETING CO.," | |

I'm not going to assume that everyone knows this: If you hover the mouse over the small square and double click on it, it will auto fill the whole column where there is data.

**Figure 2.3**  *Copying the cell by dragging down*

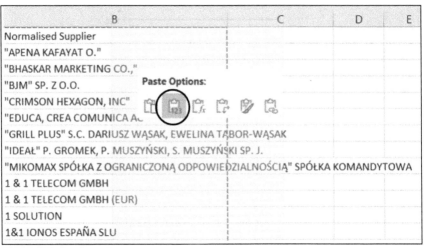

| B | C | D | E |
|---|---|---|---|
| Normalised Supplier | | | |
| "APENA KAFAYAT O." | | | |
| "BHASKAR MARKETING CO.," | | | |
| "BJM" SP. Z O.O. | | | |
| "CRIMSON HEXAGON, INC" | | | |
| "EDUCA, CREA COMUNICA A | | | |
| "GRILL PLUS" S.C. DARIUSZ WĄSAK, EWELINA TĄBOR-WĄSAK | | | |
| "IDEAŁ" P. GROMEK, P. MUSZYŃSKI, S. MUSZYŃSKI SP. J. | | | |
| "MIKOMAX SPÓŁKA Z OGRANICZONĄ ODPOWIEDZIALNOŚCIĄ" SPÓŁKA KOMANDYTOWA | | | |
| 1 & 1 TELECOM GMBH | | | |
| 1 & 1 TELECOM GMBH (EUR) | | | |
| 1 SOLUTION | | | |
| 1&1 IONOS ESPAÑA SLU | | | |

**Figure 2.4** *Pasting values*

Here are the reasons why:

INC - This is also part of the word incorporated, plus you'll find it in many other names and words in many languages, including incentives, Vincent, provincial, prince, etc. If you search and replace on Inc, it will remove it from all these names and, if you don't notice straight away, it's a lot of work and effort to fix the problem!

CO - Sometimes this is at the end of the name, or sometimes it's part of the name. It also forms part of the word 'company', amongst many others, so if you remove this accidentally and don't realise, a lot of work is required to fix the error.

LIMITED - This might seem like an unusual one, however, there are actually quite a few companies with the word 'unlimited' in their name, so if you remove the word, you are left with 'un' as part of the name.

LTD - Again, you might think that this word would be on the 'safe' list, but beware! If you are working with global data sets, there is the abbreviation LTDA for Limitada and if you remove the LTD, you are left with random As all over the data set. Sounds funny until you have to fix them!

LLC, SAS - The same as the above. These letters form parts of other names, so you are at risk of contaminating the data if you are not careful.

S.A., S.A, SA, S.L., S.L, SL - These can all be found at the start of company names as well as the end, so you have to be careful.

Sounds tricky? Fear not, there is a solution, which I'll cover later.

## Removing empty spaces

It's not just sneaky letters that can cause problems, it's the empty spaces too. The best method to use is the TRIM function; this will remove any extra spaces from the beginning, middle or end of the supplier name. To apply this, in a new column at the start of the data use the formula = TRIM(Cell number) (Figure 2.5) and that will remove any spaces (Figure 2.6).

| B | C |
|---|---|
| Normalised Supplier | |
| "APENA KAFAYAT O." | =TRIM(B2) |
| "BHASKAR    MARKETING CO.," | |
| "BJM" SP. Z O.O. | |
| "CRIMSON HEXAGON, INC" | |
| "EDUCA, CREA COMUNICA AC" | |
| "GRILL PLUS" S.C. DARIUSZ WĄSAK, EWELINA TABOR-WĄSAK | |

**Figure 2.5**  *Using the TRIM formula*

| B | C |
|---|---|
| Normalised Supplier | |
| "APENA KAFAYAT O." | "APENA KAFAYAT O." |
| "BHASKAR    MARKETING CO.," | "BHASKAR MARKETING CO.," |
| "BJM" SP. Z O.O. | "BJM" SP. Z O.O. |
| "CRIMSON HEXAGON, INC" | "CRIMSON HEXAGON, INC" |
| "EDUCA, CREA COMUNICA AC" | "EDUCA, CREA COMUNICA AC" |

**Figure 2.6**  *Example of multiple spaces*

Remember to copy over the trimmed data into the Normalised Supplier column and paste as values. As a back-up, check to make sure all the spaces have been removed. You could also do a search and replace on any double spaces – just press the spacebar twice and leave the 'Replace With' box blank.

## Normalising suppliers in Excel

There are two ways to normalise your suppliers. The first is to work in a separate sheet and use a VLOOKUP to pull back through the correct name. This is a good way if you are working with a large file and want to eliminate the chance of accidental search and replace on other parts of the file.

The second way is to work in the data as it is. However, Excel is prone to many errors, such as accidental overwrites, accidental deletions and search and replaces on the wrong data, etc., so if you can minimise these risks it's good for the integrity of the data, your sanity and saving wasted time.

For the purposes of this book, I'll show you the more foolproof version of working in a separate sheet as it's good to get in the habit of being data safe where possible. You'll need to copy over the original supplier name and the normalised name, as you'll need the original to perform the lookup once you've normalised the data.

As mentioned previously, you can't just blindly search and replace the letters you need to remove from the supplier's name. It will create more problems than you can solve, but fear not, there is a way! It's a bit fiddly working in Excel, but it is entirely possible to remove all the letters without corrupting the supplier name. I have provided a list of items to remove, carried out in a specific order, at the end of this section. Using the list, take the following steps:

1   Select and highlight the full Normalised Supplier column. This means that you'll only be searching and replacing in this column. It's important to make sure you have the column selected every time you do this - you don't want to make any changes to the original supplier name as it will affect the lookup afterwards.
2   Using the master search list (towards the end of this chapter), remove as many of the extras as possible. Excel can be sensitive to spaces and upper and lower case, so be careful to check it removes them when you perform the search and replace.
3   For those words and letters on the risky list (see page 42), you have to be extra careful. The first step is to find the words you need quickly and easily so that they can be isolated and removed safely. In a new column, use the formula =RIGHT(cell number, 4) (Figure 2.7). This will pull out the last four letters of the supplier name (Figure 2.8 opposite).

| B | C |
|---|---|
| Normalised Supplier | |
| APENA KAFAYAT O. | =right(B2,4) |
| BHASKAR MARKETING | |

**Figure 2.7** *Using the RIGHT formula*

'But words like LTD, LLC, LLP and INC are three letters long,' I hear you exclaim! Yes, that is correct, however, what if they are actually part of the supplier name and a larger word? How would you know? By adding in the

| B | C |
|---|---|
| Normalised Supplier | End |
| APENA KAFAYAT O. | T O. |
| BHASKAR MARKETING | ING |
| BJM | BJM |
| CRIMSON HEXAGON, INC | INC |
| EDUCA, CREA COMUNICA AC | A AC |
| GRILL PLUS S.C. DARIUSZ WĄSAK, EWELINA TABOR-WĄSAK | ĄSAK |
| IDEAŁ P. GROMEK, P. MUSZYŃSKI, S. MUSZYŃSKI SP. J. | . J. |
| MIKOMAX SPÓŁKA Z OGRANICZONĄ ODPOWIEDZIALNOŚCIĄ SPÓŁKA KOMAN | TOWA |
| 1 & 1 TELECOM | COM |
| 1 & 1 TELECOM | COM |
| 1 SOLUTION | TION |
| 1&1 IONOS ESPAÑA | PAÑA |
| 101 ENGINEERING | ING |
| 1010DATA, INC. DBA 1010DATA SERVICES, LLC | LLC |
| 104.COM | .COM |
| 1099EXPRESS/DALLAS | LLAS |
| 10AND5 PRODUCTIONS | IONS |
| 10DENCEHISPAHARD SL | D SL |
| 10DENCEHISPAHARD SL (CDMON) | MON) |
| 10EQS KNOWLEDGE EXCHANGE | NGE |
| 10INC. | INC. |
| 11 MADISON AVENUE LLC | LLC |

**Figure 2.8**  *Results of using the RIGHT formula*

fourth character, if it's a space, the letters will show as three characters, not four. Ta da!

You'll need to repeat this for all the other suffixes. So, if it's a four-letter suffix, you want the formula to pull back five letters, or if it's two letters, then you'd pull out three. The same principle applies however many letters you have in your suffix: always add that extra character to account for the space.

Now you have to cleanse them. Using the filter and your risky list, select your first word. In this example, I've used INC, as it's one of the words you are most likely to have issues with. The test file I'm using has a small number of suppliers; in the real-life data world you are more likely to have hundreds or thousands of results on your filter search, which is why the next part is important.

Once filtered, scroll through to check that all the suppliers have a legitimate INC to be removed. As you can see (Figure 2.9 on the next page), there's an example where INC looks like it should be part of the supplier name.

There are no fancy tricks for this. I would suggest hiding the rows that you don't need (Figure 2.10), as long as you remember to unhide them as soon as you've finished the exercise!

This is where it starts to get fiddly. When you have filters on in Excel, you can't cut and paste as you would without the filters on. If you copy (CTRL+C), as you can see, the selected cells to be copied are highlighted (Figure 2.11 opposite), but when you try to paste (CTRL+V), only the first supplier is showing. That's because the other suppliers have been pasted to hidden cells. What a potential nightmare!

| B | C |
|---|---|
| Normalised Supplier | End |
| CRIMSON HEXAGON, INC | INC |
| 10INC | 0INC |
| 1130574 ONTARIO INC | INC |
| ADT SECURITY SERVICES INC | INC |
| IBM PHILIPPINES INC | INC |
| MERCER PHILIPPINES INC | INC |
| PRICEWATERHOUSECOOPERS INC | INC |

**Figure 2.9** *Example of Inc in a supplier name*

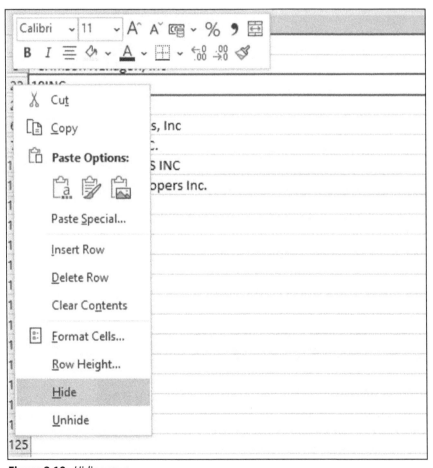

**Figure 2.10** *Hiding rows*

How do we fix this? The easiest way is to create a formula and pull through the suppliers that way. Use the formula =(the cell you want the information from) (Figure 2.12) and, again, don't cut and paste the formula down or you'll have the same issues. Instead, drag down the formula to make sure you're pulling through the correct information (Figure 2.13).

| B | | C | D |
|---|---|---|---|
| Normalised Supplier | End | | Test |
| CRIMSON HEXAGON, INC | INC | | CRIMSON HEXAGON, INC |
| 1136974 ONTARIO INC | INC | | |
| ADT SECURITY SERVICES INC | INC | | |
| IBM PHILIPPINES INC | INC | | |
| MERCER PHILIPPINES INC | INC | | |
| PRICEWATERHOUSECOOPERS INC | INC | | |

**Figure 2.11** *What happens when you copy and paste cells while on a filter*

| B | | C | D |
|---|---|---|---|
| Normalised Supplier | End | | Test |
| CRIMSON HEXAGON, INC | INC | | =B5 |
| 1136974 ONTARIO INC | INC | | |
| ADT SECURITY SERVICES INC | INC | | |
| IBM PHILIPPINES INC | INC | | |
| MERCER PHILIPPINES INC | INC | | |
| PRICEWATERHOUSECOOPERS INC | INC | | |

**Figure 2.12** *An alternative way to copy cells while on a filter*

| B | | C | D |
|---|---|---|---|
| Normalised Supplier | End | | Test |
| CRIMSON HEXAGON, INC | INC | | CRIMSON HEXAGON, INC |
| 1136974 ONTARIO INC | INC | | 1136974 ONTARIO INC |
| ADT SECURITY SERVICES INC | INC | | ADT SECURITY SERVICES INC |
| IBM PHILIPPINES INC | INC | | IBM PHILIPPINES INC |
| MERCER PHILIPPINES INC | INC | | MERCER PHILIPPINES INC |
| PRICEWATERHOUSECOOPERS INC | INC | | PRICEWATERHOUSECOOPERS INC |

**Figure 2.13** *Dragging the formula down and the results*

Then we have our next problem. The data in your new column is currently a formula so you can't do a search and replace on this – AND it's on a filter. Don't worry, I have the solution for you!

The first thing to do is clear the INC filter from the column I've named End. Once that's cleared, select the whole column I've named Test and Copy>Paste Special>Values, so that the formula is removed and the text remains where you've pulled through a name. Then you can start to search and replace for your suffixes to remove.

Start by filtering and removing the (Blanks) and this will show the companies you need to edit. Now you can see why it's important to hide those suppliers you don't need!

Select CTRL+F and carry out your search and replace on those words (Figure 2.14). Now a word of caution here: if you only had a few lines like in the example above it might be more sensible to manually delete the INC from the end of the supplier name. Sometimes the simplest options are the best; there's no need to over-engineer the process if it's not necessary.

There is an alternative to the formula =RIGHT to search for the suffixes and some of you reading this might wonder why I have not suggested it as my primary solution. The reason is that, although it might appear to be an

| | C | | D | |
|---|---|---|---|---|
| | ▾ End | | ▾ Test | ▾ |
| | INC | | CRIMSON HEXAGON, | |
| | INC | | 1136974 ONTARIO | |
| | INC | | ADT SECURITY SERVICES | |
| | INC | | IBM PHILIPPINES | |
| | INC | | MERCER PHILIPPINES | |
| | INC | | PRICEWATERHOUSECOOPERS | |

Find and Replace                                      ?    ✕

Find    Replace

Find what:    INC

Replace with:

Options >>

Replace All    Replace    Find All    Find Next    Close

Microsoft Excel                              ✕

ⓘ   All done. We made 6 replacements.

OK

**Figure 2.14** *Search and replace*

'easier' solution to some, the option of extracting the last word from every supplier has challenges of its own. The formula is =RIGHT(A2,LEN(A2)-FIND("*",SUBSTITUTE(A2," ","*",LEN(A2)-LEN(SUBSTITUTE(A2," ","")))))) and it will return the last word of the supplier, which you can then filter on and copy the supplier to another column to remove the suffixes (Figure 2.15).

This method won't, for example, pick up any suffixes that are not separated by a space or, if they are attached to another word, it will return the whole word. In large global data sets, I often find a lot of supplier names where spaces are missing, so by using this formula you would not pick up on them. You would also still have to filter and work through the suffixes from the master list, put the normalised supplier in another column and remove the suffixes from the normalised supplier name. I would therefore only recommend this option if you are short of time, with a word of warning that you might miss properly normalising the data. It's all about that A in COAT – accuracy.

It is preferable to get it as right as possible the first time. Plus, it will save time in the long run when you have an accurate master list you can confidently map to new data.

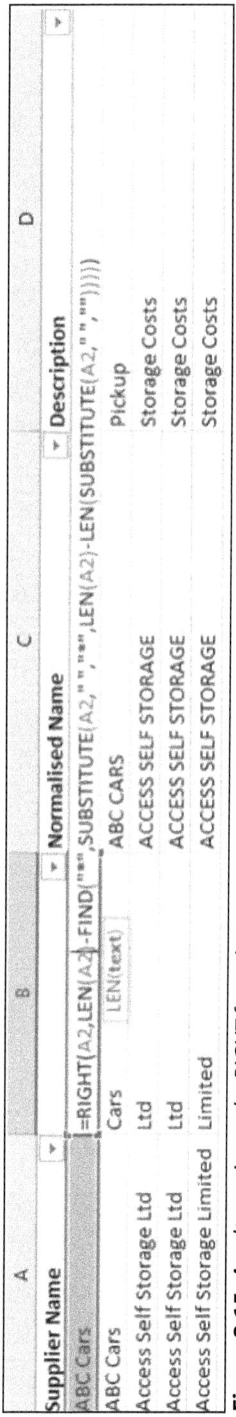

## Master search list

As previously mentioned, it's very important that you remove the suffixes in a specific order, otherwise you could end up leaving rogue commas, full stops and dashes in place. The following master search list is not exhaustive and you will have specific words in your own data file, so I would suggest scanning the list of suppliers before you start and noting any common words, characters or suffixes that you might need to remove.

**Figure 2.15** *An alternative to the RIGHT formula*

The master search list should be followed in the order it is listed to help prevent any rogue characters being left behind. You'll always find the odd one at the end of the process, but that's just the way it goes when you're working with large volumes of supplier names.

| Table 2.3 *Master search list* | | | |
|---|---|---|---|
| **ORDER OF SEARCH >>>** | | | |
| **SEARCH 1** | **SEARCH 2** | **SEARCH 3** | **SEARCH 4** |
| " | | | |
| & CO. KG. | & CO. KG | & CO KG | |
| (EUR). | (EUR) | | |
| (PTY) LTD. | (PTY) LTD | | |
| (USD). | (USD) | | |
| , INC. | , INC | INC. | INC |
| , LDA. | , LDA | LDA. | LDA |
| AB | A.B. | A.B | |
| AG | A.G. | A.G | |
| BV | B.V. | B.V | |
| BVBA. | BVBA | B.V.B.A. | B.V.B.A |
| CO., LTD. | CO., LTD | | |
| CO.LTD. | CO.LTD | | |
| CORPORATION. | CORPORATION | CORP. | CORP |
| E.K. | E.K | | |
| E.V. | E.V | | |
| EPP. | EPP | E.P.P. | E.P.P |
| GMBH + CO. KG. | GMBH + CO. KG | GMBH + CO KG | |
| G.M.B.H. | G.M.B.H | GMBH | |
| KFT. | KFT | K.F.T. | K.F.T |
| LIMITADA. | LIMITADA | | |
| LIMITED. | LIMITED | | |
| LLC. | LLC | L.L.C. | L.L.C |
| LLP. | LLP | L.L.P. | L.L.P |
| LTD. | LTD | | |
| LTDA ME. | LTDA ME | LTDA - ME | |

*Continued*

| Table 2.3 *Continued* | | | |
|---|---|---|---|
| **ORDER OF SEARCH >>>** | | | |
| **SEARCH 1** | **SEARCH 2** | **SEARCH 3** | **SEARCH 4** |
| " | | | |
| LTDA. | LTDA | | |
| ME | M.E. | M.E | |
| NV | N.V. | N.V | |
| OY | O.Y. | O.Y | |
| PTE LTD. | PTE LTD | PTE. | PTE |
| PTY LTD. | PTY LTD | PTY. | PTY |
| PVT. LTD. | PVT. LTD | PVT LTD. | PVT LTD |
| S.A. DE C.V. | S.A. DE C.V | SA DE C.V. | SA DE C.V |
| S.A.U. | S.A.U | SAU | |
| S.C. | S.C | | |
| S.L.L. | S.L.L | | |
| S.R.L | S.R.L. | | |
| S.R.O. | S.R.O | SRO | |
| SA | S.A. | S.A | |
| SA. DE CV | SA DE CV | | |
| SARL | S.A.R.L. | S.A.R.L | |
| SAS | S.A.S. | S.A.S | S A S |
| SAU | S.A.U. | S.A.U | |
| SDN. BHD. | SDN. BHD | SDN BHD. | SDN BHD |
| SL | S.L. | S.L | |
| SP. Z O.O. SP.K. | SP. Z O.O. | SP. Z O.O | SP Z.O.O |
| SPA | S.P.A. | S.P.A | |
| SPÓŁKA Z O.O. | SP ZOO | | |
| SRL | S.R.L. | S.R.L | |
| SRO | S.R.O. | S.R.O | |
| ZRT | Z.R.T. | Z.R.T | |

## Full check

Once you have removed your suffixes and any other untidy characters from the normalised supplier name, you can start to check the full list of suppliers. Create a pivot table but with the Normalised Name only. This will provide a list of unique aggregated normalised suppliers that you can

**Figure 2.16** *Pivot of normalised suppliers*

then scroll through to check for near-duplicates and correct them (Figure 2.16).

You'll also need to add a new window and arrange all vertically so that you have two tabs open together (Figure 2.17). The smaller the screen you have, the more difficult this might be, so make it work for you the best you can.

Have one tab as your pivot and the other as the raw data: that way you can view what needs to be corrected in the Pivot tab and edit in the Data tab (Figure 2.18 opposite). Once that's done, you can then hit the Refresh All button in the data tab in the ribbon at the top to update the spreadsheet.

If you look at Figure 2.18, you can see that there are two versions of Bechtle and two versions of Brakes. If you followed the TRIM function

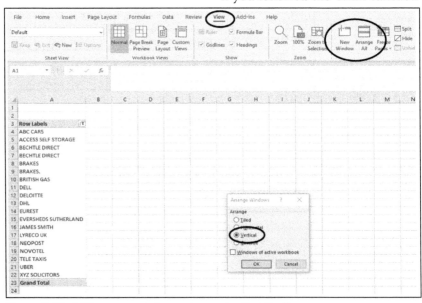

**Figure 2.17** *Adding a new window and arranging it vertically*

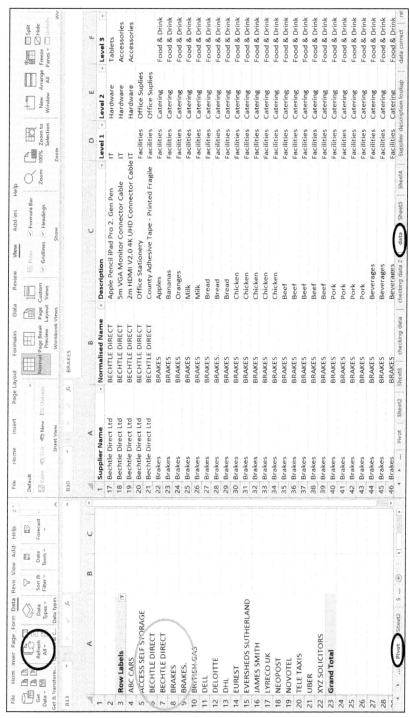

**Figure 2.18** *Arranged view vertically*

earlier, you should eradicate those pesky blanks, however, if you've made any manual adjustments, they can appear again.

You'll also notice with Brakes that a full stop has been missed during the cleansing process. I'm afraid to break it to you that I am not perfect, but because I do thorough checks of the data, my clients rarely see instances like this. This is a very small set of data; the chances are you will be working with hundreds, if not thousands of suppliers. A sensible way to work might be to do a page at a time, flipping between the Pivot and Data tabs and remembering to refresh so the pivot table updates. The last thing you want to be doing is going over data you have already corrected.

That's it, normalisation done. Right? Well, no actually. Remember I told you I'm thorough? Once you have been through the full list of suppliers and made changes, you need to go through it again. Why? Because by correcting and updating the data, you might inadvertently create new near-duplicates. For example, if you have corrected THE HILTON HOTEL to HILTON HOTEL, when you rework the normalised list you might find that all the other Hilton Hotels are normalised to HILTON HOTELS plural, and then you have two versions of Hilton. This can happen quite often, so as painful an exercise as it is, it is worth it in the long run as you are helping to build a great, accurate data set that can be used as a master for future refreshes.

| Supplier Name | Normalised Name | Description |
|---|---|---|
| ABC Cars | =VLOOKUP(A2,'Master norm'!$A:$B,2,0) | Taxi |
| ABC Cars | | Pickup |
| Access Self Storage Ltd | | Storage Costs |
| Access Self Storage Ltd | | Storage Costs |
| Access Self Storage Limited | | Storage Costs |
| Access Self Storage | | Storage Costs |
| Access Self Storage | | Storage Costs |

Figure 2.19 Using a VLOOKUP formula

We still need to apply these beautifully normalised supplier names back into the full data set. This can be done with the VLOOKUP formula (Figure 2.19, facing page), looking up on the original supplier name, and pulling through the normalised name from the new tab or spreadsheet you have been working in (Figure 2.20).

| A Supplier Name | B Normalised Name | C Description |
|---|---|---|
| ABC Cars | ABC CARS | Taxi |
| ABC Cars | ABC CARS | Pickup |
| Access Self Storage Ltd | ACCESS SELF STORAGE | Storage Costs |
| Access Self Storage Ltd | ACCESS SELF STORAGE | Storage Costs |
| Access Self Storage Limited | ACCESS SELF STORAGE | Storage Costs |
| Access Self Storage | ACCESS SELF STORAGE | Storage Costs |
| Access Self Storage | ACCESS SELF STORAGE | Storage Costs |
| Access Self Storage Limited | ACCESS SELF STORAGE | Storage Costs |
| Access Self Storage Ltd | ACCESS SELF STORAGE | Storage Costs |
| Access Self Storage Ltd | ACCESS SELF STORAGE | Storage Costs |
| Bechtle Direct Ltd | BECHTLE DIRECT | County Adhesive Tape - Printed Fragile |
| Bechtle Direct Ltd | BECHTLE DIRECT | Office Stationery |
| Bechtle Direct Ltd | BECHTLE DIRECT | 2m HDMI V2.0 4K UHD Connector Cable |
| Bechtle Direct Ltd | BECHTLE DIRECT | 5m VGA Monitor Connector Cable |
| Bechtle Direct Ltd | BECHTLE DIRECT | Apple Pencil iPad Pro 2. Gen Pen |
| Bechtle Direct Ltd | BECHTLE DIRECT | Apple Pencil iPad Pro 2. Gen Pen |
| Bechtle Direct Ltd | BECHTLE DIRECT | 5m VGA Monitor Connector Cable |
| Bechtle Direct Ltd | BECHTLE DIRECT | 2m HDMI V2.0 4K UHD Connector Cable |
| Bechtle Direct Ltd | BECHTLE DIRECT | Office Stationery |
| Bechtle Direct Ltd | BECHTLE DIRECT | County Adhesive Tape - Printed Fragile |

**Figure 2.20** *Results of using the VLOOKUP formula*

Even though you have already spent time normalising and making that list perfect, it's always worth checking that the VLOOKUP has pulled through correctly. You wouldn't want your hard work to be tainted by a bad formula! When you are confident that it has, remember to copy that column and paste as values.

## Automating normalisation in Excel

If you are maintaining your data regularly and updating it with new normalisation, a fast and efficient way to do this is by creating a master file from the existing normalised data set.

Firstly, create a pivot table with the supplier name and the normalised name so that you get a unique list of the original supplier name with the assigned normalised name. This is important because you'll be using a VLOOKUP to find the supplier name and if there are multiple versions of the same name, it will take the first value. If you've missed correcting an error in the checking process, you could potentially incorrectly normalise a supplier for many refreshes before it's realised.

As you can see from Figure 2.21 below, the pivot table has aggregated and listed the normalised supplier name Brakes twice. The reason in this instance is that I missed that pesky full stop again, but because I'm thorough, nearly all these things get picked up before it goes back to my client, or as it could be in your case, the rest of the business.

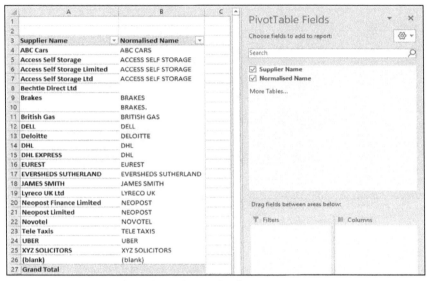

**Figure 2.21** *Aggregated supplier and normalised name using a pivot*

The next step is to add view and arrange all vertically, having the pivot table and raw data side by side, making sure you do a sweep to correct anything that isn't right in the raw data tab. Remember to refresh the data in your pivot tab so that you're not going over suppliers you've already corrected.

Once you're confident, copy this pivot table into a new file and call it something like the 'Master Norm' or 'Master Normalisation' file. When that next set of data needs to be normalised, use a VLOOKUP to pull through the normalised names from the master file, matching on the original supplier name. If you work in a company, I would hope that 80-90% of the names should get normalised as I wouldn't expect your organisation's new suppliers or variations of the same suppliers to increase that much between refreshes.

This should leave you only a small number of entries to update. If you're lucky and it is a small number, you can either manually update them or in a new column use the =UPPER formula to create the names in upper case, copy and paste them as values and then work on cleaning the suffixes in that column before adding them into the normalised name column via a VLOOKUP (as we've already covered). Finally, as always, PASTE AS VALUES! Was that clear enough? I think so!

Now that you have some new names for your master norm file, there's a couple of ways to approach this. You could filter on the column that you've been working in to update the missing normalised names, as long as you haven't copied the =UPPER formula through the whole column. If you haven't, you can filter out the blanks and just copy the list of supplier and normalised names into your master norm file.

If you have used the =UPPER formula on the whole column, you'll need to copy all the supplier and normalised names into the master file. Either way, once the new names have been added to the master norm list, it's good practice to create a pivot table from that and go through the previous steps to check for any near-duplicates that the new suppliers you have added may have caused.

When you have finished checking this and are happy, copy this new unique list into a new file and make this your new master norm file, archiving or deleting any older versions.

## Conclusion

That is normalisation, my friends. Hopefully you've picked up from this chapter that the secret to fantastically accurate normalised names is the well known 'rinse and repeat' method. Checking your supplier names once is not enough, and if you have thousands, or tens of thousands of suppliers, a lot can slip through the net.

By using the risky and master lists I've provided to search for suffixes, you will have improved normalised suppliers, as well as more accurate reporting and visualisation on things like spend by supplier and sales by customer. Plus, you can rationalise your supplier base without even having to delete any suppliers – magic!

By doing two to three checks of your data, you will iron out the majority of the issues in the file. I *want* you to put me out of a job, I *want* you to take ownership and beautifully manicure and maintain that data of yours and I'm giving you the tools to do it.

# 3 Taxonomies

## What is a taxonomy?

According to *Collins Dictionary* (2021), the definition of a taxonomy is 'the process of naming and classifying things such as animals and plants into groups within a larger system, according to their similarities and differences'.

That's a very broad and vague description and I'd say a taxonomy is more than that. In my spend classification world, a taxonomy is a list of categories and sub-categories used to classify data into groups or 'buckets' of items or services, providing a unified view for the purpose of reporting and analytics. It can be used by the whole business or just one department, such as procurement. In procurement, a taxonomy can also be known as a 'category' or 'spend tree'.

You might not realise it, but taxonomies are used in many everyday activities, for example online shopping. Every time you do your online food shop, you are inadvertently using a taxonomy. If you need to search for apples, you might go to Fresh Food, followed by Fruit, followed by Apples. That's your level 1, 2 and 3. Try looking on another supermarket's website and you'll find the apples in a different category structure.

This is reflective of spend taxonomies in business too. You'll find many different variations, all being used with differing perspectives. If you move from company A to company B, you might find that everything you knew is now different in your new company.

A taxonomy usually has several levels and the number can range from 1-6 (although I have heard of more, can you believe?!). I would recommend 3-4 levels as the optimal option, the reason being that most organisations do not interrogate their data to any further level of detail. Also, the more detailed the taxonomy, the longer the classification process takes and the more open it is to mistakes.

Think of peripherals: if you can classify mouse, keyboard, monitor and docking station all as peripherals, you can classify that pretty quickly. However, if you have to search for each item individually, and classify it individually, it adds time to the process.

A more complex example could be lab chemicals. If you classify everything as lab chemicals, that will take significantly less time than if you have to separate them out by the types of chemical. If you're not familiar with what they are, you might need to spend time on Google finding out what they are before you can classify them.

It's important to think about the benefit to your business of having that level of detail. Do you need it? Will you use it? Will this take longer to classify and/or put people off classifying properly?

If you want something simple, I suggest it should look something like this:

| Table 3.1 *Example of a simple taxonomy* | | | |
|---|---|---|---|
| **Level 1** | **Level 2** | **Level 3** | **Level 4** |
| Facilities | Cleaning | Cleaning Services | |
| Facilities | Cleaning | Cleaning Consumables | |
| HR | Recruitment | Temporary | |
| HR | Recruitment | Permanent | |
| IT | Hardware | Laptops | |
| IT | Hardware | Peripherals | Keyboard |
| Professional Services | Legal Services | | |

I have seen some incredibly complex taxonomies, such as ones that use a combination of letters fed from multiple tables based on information such as location, description and product type. People within that organisation who have worked there for some time can understand what the classification is just by looking at the codes, but it can be very difficult for those without that knowledge to understand or categorise the data properly.

From a spend analytics perspective, I believe a taxonomy should be descriptive and have words/categories representing the spend in the company that could be understood by anyone from inside or outside the organisation.

## Why do I need a taxonomy? Why not use GL codes?

We touched on GL codes in Chapter 1 - The Dangers of Dirty Data. These codes are used by finance/accounting departments to track financial transactions, but the code can be a product, service or even a project, so it's not necessarily the right categorisation for other parts of the business. In my experience, when classifying spend data and a GL code is part of the data set, more often than not that GL code is incorrect or misleading.

Think back to the example used in Chapter 1, the client of mine where I classified their data. For the first time, they had visibility on their spend across the whole business globally. When we looked at one particular supplier, the classification was under car leasing, but the client had four different GL codes assigned to them, ranging from office supplies to employee benefits. This raised a lot of questions for the client: Were the GL codes correct? What was the logic in assigning these specific codes? Did they need to review them?

From an accounting perspective, the codes could have been correct, however, from a procurement perspective, this information was incorrect. It would have given a misleading picture to procurement and could have potentially led to the wrong decisions being made.

Another example could be that the marketing department needs some leaflets printed for a new campaign, but they have used up all their budget. They talk to their friends in the sales department and ask if they have some spare budget and can put the spend through under their budget code instead. Sales agree and so that spend is now sitting under 'sales' in the general ledger. If a spend taxonomy had been used to classify it, this would not happen. The taxonomy classification represents a product or service bought, sold or used within the company, and that classification will not change, regardless of which department uses or needs it.

For example, in the scenario I've described in the paragraph above, by using a spend taxonomy, the supplier that the print was bought from would be classified as print; it would have no affiliation with a specific business department, so the classification would remain unchanged, regardless of who used it. This is also better from a spend management perspective, as the procurement manager would want to see all the print spend in once place. This could only be achieved by using a taxonomy, as some of the spend could be hidden in an unidentifiable GL code.

So, if you can avoid using GL codes, I'm begging you, for your own procurement data accuracy, please do it!

## What is a good/bad taxonomy?
### Good taxonomies
I have seen the good, the bad and the ugly of taxonomies in my decade working with spend data, so I'm in a great position to help guide you through this mysterious world.

A good taxonomy will be consistent. What I mean by that is that there will be a common structure throughout all the categories. If you have four levels of detail in IT, you should also have the same in office supplies, which sits under facilities. For example, if you're going to classify to the level of computers, peripherals and printers in IT, this should also be reflected in office supplies with paper, desk supplies and ink cartridges. However, if you only have hardware in IT, then you would only need office supplies or stationery in facilities.

Ideally, your taxonomy should have no more than 15 categories at Level 1. Senior management like to view reports at top level and if you have any more categories than this at Level 1 it makes reporting very difficult. Too many categories and it stops being top-level information!

Below are some options for what a Level 1 taxonomy could look like:

| Table 3.2 *Options for a Level 1 taxonomy* | | |
|---|---|---|
| **Option 1** | | **Option 2** |
| LEVEL 1 | | LEVEL 1 |
| Direct | | Facilities |
| Indirect | | HR |
| Non-Addressable | | IT |
| | | Laboratory |
| | | Marketing |
| | | MRO |
| | | Professional Services |
| | | Raw Materials |
| | | Telecoms |
| | | Travel |

A good taxonomy will also reflect the quality of the data you have. You might *want* to classify down to a keyboard level of detail in your IT spend, but do you have that level of detail in the data, or can you only go as far as peripheral or hardware?

It's important to manage expectations and keep your classification accurate by only having options in the taxonomy that are appropriate and suitable. Otherwise, you will end up with a whole lot of spend classified under keyboards that shouldn't be there because someone 'thinks' that's what you spent it on. Always follow the detail in the data.

Your taxonomy also needs to be relevant. Do you have all the options that you need? I have seen key areas of spend missing from taxonomies, such as tax, memberships, subscriptions, online marketing/social media, donations, sponsorship, road tolls, parking and gifts. When things like this are missing, the items are then shoehorned into a vaguely relevant category that doesn't actually reflect the true spend or usage of the item.

You might think that some of these things are not a priority or that important, but I can promise you, all the little costs, such as tolls and parking, can soon add up over the course of a year. This can all lead to misinformation, incorrect classification and potentially bad business decisions.

I also see a lot of taxonomies that use company-specific terminology or acronyms. You should avoid this if possible. A good taxonomy should be able to be understood and used by those external to the organisation, as well as those within it. This minimises the risk of incorrect classification or misinterpretation. I was working on a project where there was a reference to the '3Cs' in a meeting. I had to clarify what they were referring to as when I googled the definition, there were multiple options. That is why simplicity and clarity work best in taxonomies.

A good taxonomy will also be analytics friendly. Don't have long and wordy descriptions that will be cut off or hard to read when you build a chart. Keep them short, succinct and easy to interpret - all chart-friendly traits so that they are not bigger or longer than the chart itself.  A chart is only as good as the information that feeds into it, and that includes the descriptions.

## Bad taxonomies

Rarely is it obvious at first sight that a taxonomy is a bad taxonomy, but if it's only a one or two-level taxonomy with just a few rows and limited options, it is more likely to be unfit for purpose. On the flip side, if it's too detailed, it can also cause confusion and misclassification.

A bad taxonomy hinders more than it helps. It can lead to misinformation, incorrect data and, ultimately, bad business decisions, potentially costing an organisation money, jobs or worse. It sounds dramatic but it's true. These consequences are an important consideration when you are working with a taxonomy.

Taxonomies can be too wordy, like in the examples on the next page. This confuses those using the taxonomy by making them think that the spend has to be very specific for it to fit into that category. More often than not, it then ends up in the wrong category because it doesn't fit their expectations.

I'll cover this further in Chapter 4 - Spend Data Classification, but classification is already a subjective activity. There can often be more than one right answer (remember COAT - keep it consistent) so if you can minimise the opportunity for people to make the wrong decision, it will benefit everyone in the long run. Remember, it might not always be

| **Table 3.3** *Examples of poor and good descriptions* | |
|---|---|
| POOR DESCRIPTIONS | GOOD DESCRIPTIONS |
| Information Technology Services and Equipment and Accessories | IT |
| Human Resources and Employee Related | HR |
| Lubricants and Fuels and Additives | Fuels & Lubricants |
| Maintenance and Repair and Operations | MRO |
| Travel and Road Transportation and Accommodation | Travel |

someone experienced in classification working with the taxonomy, so by making it as clear and simple as possible, it helps everyone.

For example, what if you have a currency exchange fee for an employee when travelling on business, but because this is not listed in the poor Level 1 description, you might think it shouldn't sit there, and so you put it under Financial Services. It's not a bad option, but it is not right for employee expenses. By keeping it broad and simply having the first level as Travel, it leaves wide-ranging options to classify the spend data and it is more likely to end up in the right category. You can then close in on the detail in Level 2 and beyond.

## Off-the-shelf versus custom

It is easy to reach for a ready-made, ready-to-use taxonomy. There are many out there, including UNSPSC, eClass, Proclass and Proc-HE, to name a few. There's an element of trust and familiarity, like your favourite old pair of slippers. They are established, well used and widely known taxonomies that many people are familiar with and they cross organisations and industries.

Whilst it's an easy option to choose one of these taxonomies, I would describe them as like ready-to-wear clothing. It aims to fit the general population and so when you buy a dress or suit off the rack, maybe it's too big on the top or the trousers are too long. You either have to wear it like it is or spend more money on a tailor to get it to fit comfortably.

An off-the-shelf taxonomy is exactly the same. It might have most of what you need, possibly a lot of what you don't, but more importantly, there could be key areas missing. As a result, spend is shoehorned into a vaguely relevant category and you might not even realise until you spot gaps in your classification through analytics, which could be months, even years later. Think how much data will have been classified by then.

If you build a customised taxonomy, it will fit your data perfectly. If you work in an industry with niche or specific products, this will give you the visibility that would just not be possible with an off-the-shelf taxonomy. It does require a level of skill, knowledge and patience to create a customised taxonomy, but there are professionals who can do this for you.

## Why is a customised taxonomy better?

A customised taxonomy will cover all the categories you need to classify your data. From a procurement/spend management perspective, this means that you are accurately representing what your organisation is buying from its suppliers. It allows you to accurately measure things like spend by supplier, number of invoices per supplier and compliance of spend on- or off-contract, use it for contract renegotiations and, finally, the best bit – cost savings.

There is a middle option – modifying an off-the-shelf taxonomy, however, I've only ever seen a Frankenstein effect with this. Quite often it's been modified by someone with little experience in taxonomies and it lacks consistency with the rest of the taxonomy, which in turn has a knock-on effect of what I can only describe as wonky reporting and analytics.

## How to build a spend taxonomy

It might seem intimidating at first, but most taxonomies start with the same core Level 1s, such as Facilities, and then, depending on your industry, you might need to add in some specific to your needs. Once you have your Level 1s, it gets easier for the Level 2s. Depending on your organisation, some Level 2s will sit under different Level 1s.

A great example is IT or HR consultancy. I've seen it sit under IT/HR and I've also seen it under Professional Services, and I've even heard of it sitting in both! I'll cover this more in Chapter 4, but it is imperative that you have one classification for each item – think COAT: Consistent, Organised, Accurate and Trustworthy. Whichever category you choose, stick to that one and make sure the same option is not available elsewhere in the taxonomy.

The level of detail in your data will determine whether you need Levels 3 or 4 of the taxonomy. If you are classifying at supplier level only, then you only need a 2–3 level taxonomy as without detail it would be hard to be specific about the spend. For example, you'll only be able to classify IT spend to hardware at best, and office supplies as stationery.

If you have very detailed invoice descriptions, then you can go to town with the detail, within reason. Industries such as manufacturing, pharmaceuticals and education tend to have lots of detailed invoice descriptions as they are buying in lots of parts, chemicals, lab supplies, stationery or crafts products.

However, be careful not to go into too much detail in your taxonomy for every item. If you have a number of rows for some serological pipettes or a flat head screw for example, it would be appropriate to have a categorisation for this in the taxonomy. If you only have one row in your data for a socket screw, then it would be more appropriate to classify this to the level above, which would be screws.

That's why it's important to build the taxonomy as you classify the data. You can start with a skeleton taxonomy using the suggested levels I've given you, but it's really important to add and modify this as you work with the data. There's no shortcut for this; it has to be done by someone who is familiar with procurement data or by category specialists.

## Conclusion

A good taxonomy will fit the needs of your business. It will be consistent and it will reflect the quality of the data you have, for example, if there is detail and the business requires it, you would have a detailed taxonomy across all levels. Make sure the options are appropriate and suitable and that they will be relevant (without acronyms if possible) to minimise misclassification.

Finally, think about how the categories will translate into analytics. Will they be chart-friendly with clear descriptions that are easy to read and interpret? This will also help with classification, about which you will find out more in the next chapter.

# 4 Spend Data Classification

## What is spend data classification?

My background is specifically in spend data classification and working with procurement teams, so this is where my knowledge and experience comes from. Whatever area of data you work in, this chapter will give you information and tips to help you work more efficiently and accurately.

Turning to trusty Google to get a definition for spend data classification, the first thing that came up was my very own definition! My definition states that spend data classification is the categorisation of financial data into groups or 'buckets' of spend using a taxonomy or category tree.

The next best definition I found was from the cloud-based spend analytics solution Accelerated Insight (2021), which states 'Spend Data Classification is the process of grouping spend data for similar goods or services, assigning them to predefined categories using a Taxonomy document'.

If I broaden the search to data classification, which covers a much wider range of different types of classification, Technopedia provides a good definition:

> Data classification is the process of sorting and categorising data into various types, forms or any other distinct class. Data classification enables the separation and classification of data according to data set requirements for various business or personal objectives. It is mainly a data management process.
>
> (Technopedia, 2021)

My definition of data classification would be similar to my definition of spend data: data classification is the categorisation of data into groups or 'buckets' using a taxonomy. I want to define spend data classification in business terms, not technical terms. The biggest area of error in data comes from people inputting data/information who are not experts in the field and are intimidated by the technical terms used when working with data.

Spend data classification requires a different skill and knowledge base than master data classification, because classifying spend data is subjective and very much depends on the context. Rarely is there a black or white, yes or no answer in spend data classification. There can be multiple correct answers for the same supplier and it's all about agreeing to those standards internally, especially if you have multiple people working on the data.

Having managed a team of 14 people, I know how hard it is to maintain that consistency. What helped me was to provide them with a list of common suppliers and a standard classification for them. That's where COAT came from - making sure your data is Consistent, Accurate, Organised and Trustworthy.

Think of it this way; your data is much easier to fix if you have everything classified the same but incorrect, rather than having multiple classifications against one supplier/description and having to spend time going through finding them and correcting the classification. It's very frustrating and time-consuming and, depending on the level of complexity, sometimes it's easier just to start again.

## Classification best practice

Let's start with the basics.

The most important thing to keep in mind when you are classifying spend data is to think about what the company you are working for, or classifying the data for, would buy from this supplier. This is so important. There are a number of examples I can give you where taking the information at face value will lead to incorrect classification, dirty data and bad decision making.

The second most important thing is to look at the supplier name and invoice/PO description in context.

## Supplier names

A supplier name on its own will not give you enough information. Think of Wal-Mart: you could be buying fuel, food, furniture or office supplies. How can you be accurate in your classification with so little information? It's the same with Amazon. Are you buying clothing, electricals, furniture, office supplies or web hosting services? The possibilities are endless and so you need further information to guide you.

When negotiating with suppliers, you need to make sure your information is as accurate as possible so you can negotiate the best pricing for whatever it is you are buying. How can you negotiate with Wal-Mart or Amazon if you don't know what you're buying? There could be tens, if not hundreds, if not millions of pounds/euros/dollars to be saved, but you'll never know if you don't have the data.

## Invoice/PO descriptions

On the flip side of this is the invoice/PO description. You might have a description such as service, but if you don't look at that in context with the supplier name, how will you know what the service is? If the supplier name is XYZ consultants, then it's classified as professional services; if it's ABC cleaning then it's a facilities classification; and if it's 123 Computer Services then it's an IT classification.

Using both the supplier name and invoice or PO description is key to accurate data classification. Remember way back in Chapter 1 - The Dangers of Dirty Data when I discussed the issue I had with a new team member who had classified LinkedIn, the incredibly well known business networking and training platform, as a restaurant because the description said restaurant? Not only is this an incorrect classification, but if it's not picked up, it will have an effect on the credibility of your work or that of your department, rendering your data untrustworthy. Your data is left without its COAT on, because you can't have trustworthy data without it being consistent, accurate and organised.

## Context

As I've said, in spend data classification not everything is as it seems and here are some great examples. Firstly, let's think about ABC Consultancy. They have several invoice line descriptions:

**Table 4.1**  *Examples of invoice line descriptions*

| Supplier Name | Normalised Supplier | Invoice Description | Amount |
|---|---|---|---|
| ABD Consultancy Ltd. | ABC CONSULTANCY | Services 01/03-10/03 | 5,000.00 |
| ABD Consultancy Ltd. | ABC CONSULTANCY | Services 01/02-10/02 | 5,000.00 |
| ABD Consultancy Ltd. | ABC CONSULTANCY | Hotel | 250.00 |
| ABD Consultancy Ltd. | ABC CONSULTANCY | Taxi | 15.00 |

If you look at this from a description perspective only, the hotel and taxi could end up getting classified as travel. But if we look at this in context with the supplier name, the picture changes. As I said at the start of this chapter, think about what the company you are working for or classifying data for would be buying from this supplier. Would they be buying a hotel room or taxi from ABC Consultancy? If the answer is no, it should not be classified as travel. In this particular example, it is easier to decide what to classify it as, because the hint is in the supplier name – Consultancy. You might find that a lot of consultants appear as just a person's name and it could look more like an employee expense, which would legitimately be travel.

How can you tell the difference? Context is key. If you just look at the individual row of that supplier, the picture tells you that this looks like an employee travel expense:

**Table 4.2**  *A supplier viewed as an individual row*

| Supplier Name | Normalised Supplier | Invoice Description | Amount |
|---|---|---|---|
| John Smith | JOHN SMITH | Hotel | 250.00 |

However, if you look at ALL the supplier rows together, context kicks in and a very different picture appears:

**Table 4.3**  *A supplier viewed with all their rows*

| Supplier Name | Normalised Supplier | Invoice Description | Amount |
|---|---|---|---|
| John Smith | JOHN SMITH | Services 01/03-10/03 | 5,000.00 |
| John Smith | JOHN SMITH | Services 01/02-10/02 | 5,000.00 |
| John Smith | JOHN SMITH | Hotel | 250.00 |
| John Smith | JOHN SMITH | Taxi | 15.00 |

You might be thinking that you wouldn't be looking at a single row of supplier data on its own; however, with the methodology I'm going to show you, this will happen and that's why it's important that you do spot checks at the end of classifying your data, as I've shown you in Chapter 1 – The Dangers of Dirty Data.

## Other common classification errors

Another example of where common classification errors happen is around deliveries. Again, think about what the company you are classifying for would be buying from that supplier. If the description is delivery, carriage or freight, is that supplier a courier or logistics company? If not, you need to classify it as part of the product you have bought. You should not have any delivery charges as part of a service, and if you do, I would double-check that as it's not a good sign.

Here's a good example:

**Table 4.4** *Classification errors involving delivery*

| Supplier Name | Normalised Supplier | Invoice Description | Amount |
|---|---|---|---|
| Dell Inc | DELL | Server | 10,000.00 |
| Dell Ltd | DELL | Laptop | 5,000.00 |
| Dell Computers | DELL | Delivery | 150.00 |
| Dell Software | DELL | Software | 10,000.00 |

If you buy a computer from Dell, the delivery will be included as a separate line on the invoice. This does not mean you have paid them for a delivery service; the charge is part of the cost of the products that you have purchased from this supplier. In this instance, you could classify to the level of IT > Hardware at best, but this is still more accurate than a delivery or courier classification.

Think back to that shower gel analogy. All those small delivery charges don't look much as individual rows of data, but combined across a number of suppliers over the course of a year or more it could lead to a significant amount of spend being classified in the wrong place, again leading to potentially bad business decisions.

There's one more example I want to share with you that's more of a grey area and would need to be decided within your business and what works best for them: maintenance services. Whether it be plumbing or electrical or MRO (Maintenance, Repair & Operations) equipment maintenance, the supplier could be an electrician or electrical contractor, or mechanical engineer, but they may have to supply parts to fix something. This is where the dilemma comes in. Do you classify the parts as specific parts, which might sit under a different category, or do you classify it as part of the service?

Here is a common example of what you might find:

**Table 4.5** *Classification errors involving maintenance*

| Supplier Name | Normalised Supplier | Invoice Description | Amount |
|---|---|---|---|
| ZZZ Electrical Ltd | ZZZ ELECTRICAL | Services | 500.00 |
| ZZZ Electrical Ltd | ZZZ ELECTRICAL | Parts | 25.00 |
| ZZZ Electrical Ltd | ZZZ ELECTRICAL | Fuses | 10.00 |
| ZZZ Electrical Ltd | ZZZ ELECTRICAL | Maintenance | 450.00 |

In some instances, it might not be possible to classify parts as the description is too vague, but if you do have detail, what should you do? Personally, I work to the rule of classifying all of the above as Facilities > Electrical Services, the reason being that procurement is looking at influenceable spend and products or services they can negotiate on and make cost savings.

With this example, the electrician is supplying the parts that they will have already pre-bought at a specific price. Procurement would not have the ability to have any influence over the price of any of the parts unless they decide to buy and stock the parts needed from the manufacturer or distributor directly, but then how would they know what parts they needed? It would be too complicated and require too much storage space. What is influenceable is the electrician's service fees and these can be negotiated. That's why I would classify it all as Electrical Services.

All these examples come from my years of experience in classifying data, but there could be circumstances where these suggestions are not right for your business or situation. You should always check and agree with the decision makers and data users first. It's back to COAT and making sure you are consistent in processes and classification standards.

## GL codes

Let's talk about GL codes. You've heard me talk emphatically about using invoice and PO descriptions to guide you in your classification, but you might be thinking, 'we use GL codes in our company'. I touched on this ever so slightly in Chapters 1 and 3 but would like to emphasise again how much I do not trust GL codes when it comes to spend data classification.

I always tell my team that they should only ever use these as a very, very, very last resort for classification and if all other options have failed. GL codes are used from a finance perspective, which means they could be assigned to projects as well as specific items, which is not helpful from a procurement perspective. They can be very misleading, too generic or project based rather than product or service based, which means you could end up misclassifying the data.

I used the example in earlier chapters of four GL codes assigned to a car lease company, ranging from office expenses to employee benefits. This is what I would class as an obvious example. Think of all the suppliers out there where it might not be obvious what product or service they provide and have been assigned a misleading GL code, either because it's been assigned incorrectly or because it's been assigned from a finance perspective.

If the procurement function is blindly trusting the GL code for guidance on spend, the results versus correct spend data classification could vary hugely. That's missed cost savings and missed opportunities to rationalise suppliers, monitor spend and contract compliance correctly and even check for fraudulent activity.

We tend to trust that finance will be accurate and we can rely on their data. However, just like spend data classification, assigning a GL code can be very subjective, which is why you end up with multiple GL codes against one supplier, like the car lease company example.

If you are only using GL codes to manage your spend currently, you can use the spot-checking method I shared with you in Chapter 1 to check how many GL codes are assigned to a single supplier. This should at least help you make a decision on whether you can trust the GL codes you have or whether you might want to consider classifying your spend data with either an off-the-shelf or a customised taxonomy.

## Classifying data in Excel

Let's go back to the very beginning. You open your fresh new spreadsheet with supplier name, description, amount and perhaps some other columns, along with your taxonomy levels, all ready to classify. If this is a brand new set of data, start reading from this point. If you are working on a refresh and are updating the data, head to the next section, 'Updating new data with existing classified data', first before embarking on this step.

As with normalisation, it is so important that you don't overwrite existing data. If you need to create extra columns for anything you might need, do so, but with the exception of the classification columns, which might already exist and have some data. The next stage, again as with normalisation, hide any of the columns you don't need. I like to try and fit all my columns into one screen so I'm not scrolling or flicking between things. That might be harder with smaller screens but generally the columns I need to classify are the original supplier name, the normalised name, the invoice/PO description columns, the GL code (to be used very cautiously) and the amount or value column.

## Common words in spend data

There are two stages to the classification process, both using what I refer to as 'quick wins'. The first is to search normalised supplier names for recognisable keywords or familiar/recognisable company names that might come up in the data.

If you work for a company and are working with the same data regularly, you can quickly build up your own list of 'quick wins'. If you are constantly working with different data sets, the best thing to do is scan the list of supplier names and look for common words. Within each industry, these will be different, but you can start to build a list for each industry as I can guarantee the same suppliers will come up.

Below is a list of common words and companies that you might come across while classifying spend data. As you might be working with global data sets, I've included other languages and region-specific items that I commonly find in global data sets.

**Table 4.6** *Common words and companies found when classifying spend data*

| Word | Classification | | Word | Classification | |
|---|---|---|---|---|---|
| Pitney Bowes | Facilities | Franking Machine | Caterer | Facilities | Catering |
| DHL | Facilities | Post & Courier | Catering | Facilities | Catering |
| DPD | Facilities | Post & Courier | Cleaning | Facilities | Cleaning |
| Federal Express | Facilities | Post & Courier | Limpeza | Facilities | Cleaning |
| Fedex | Facilities | Post & Courier | Canon | Facilities | Copier Rental |
| United Parcel Service | Facilities | Post & Courier | Xerox | Facilities | Copier Rental |
| UPS | Facilities | Post & Courier | Shred-IT | Facilities | Document Destruction |
| Yodel | Facilities | Post & Courier | Iron Mountain | Facilities | Document Management |
| Floral | HR | Gifts | Electrical | Facilities | Electrical Services |
| Florist | HR | Gifts | Air Con | Facilities | HVAC |
| Flowers | HR | Gifts | HVAC | Facilities | HVAC |
| Recruitment | HR | Recruitment | Furniture | Facilities | Office Furniture |
| Resources | HR | Recruitment | Pest | Facilities | Pest Control |
| Staffing | HR | Recruitment | Pest Control | Facilities | Pest Control |
| City of | Tax | | Plumber | Facilities | Plumbing Services |
| Comptroller | Tax | | Plumbing | Facilities | Plumbing Services |
| Council | Tax | | Property | Facilities | Rent |
| Stadt | Tax | | Realty | Facilities | Rent |
| State | Tax | | Fire | Facilities | Security |
| Car Rental | Travel | Car Hire | Security | Facilities | Security |

*Continued*

**Table 4.6** *Continued*

| Word | Classification | | Word | Classification | |
|---|---|---|---|---|---|
| Rent a Car | Travel | Car Hire | Energy | Facilities | Utilities |
| Aer Lingus | Travel | Flights | Gas | Facilities | Utilities |
| Air Canada | Travel | Flights | Water | Facilities | Utilities |
| American Airlines | Travel | Flights | Aquaid | Facilities | Watercoolers |
| British Airways | Travel | Flights | Eden Springs | Facilities | Watercoolers |
| Delta | Travel | Flights | Watercoolers Direct | Facilities | Watercoolers |
| Easyjet | Travel | Flights | Waterlogic | Facilities | Watercoolers |
| Iberia | Travel | Flights | Pertemps | HR | Temporary Recruitment |
| Ryanair | Travel | Flights | Software | IT | Software |
| Southwest Airlines | Travel | Flights | Creative | Marketing | Creative |
| United Airlines | Travel | Flights | Events | Marketing | Event Management |
| Virgin Atlantic | Travel | Flights | Association | Marketing | Memberships |
| Accor | Travel | Hotel | Chamber of Commerce | Marketing | Memberships |
| Best Western | Travel | Hotel | Chambre de Commerce | Marketing | Memberships |
| Hilton | Travel | Hotel | Photographer | Marketing | Photography |
| Holiday Inn | Travel | Hotel | Photography | Marketing | Photography |
| Hotel | Travel | Hotel | Print | Marketing | Print |
| Hyatt | Travel | Hotel | Translations | Marketing | Translations |
| Inn | Travel | Hotel | Consultancy | Professional Services | Consulting |
| Lodge | Travel | Hotel | Consultant | Professional Services | Consulting |
| Mariott | Travel | Hotel | Consulting | Professional Services | Consulting |
| Marriot | Travel | Hotel | Accountants | Professional Services | Financial Services |
| Marriott | Travel | Hotel | Accounting | Professional Services | Financial Services |
| Radisson | Travel | Hotel | Advocat | Professional Services | Legal Services |
| Shangri La | Travel | Hotel | Avocat | Professional Services | Legal Services |

*Continued*

**Table 4.6** *Continued*

| Word | Classification | | Word | Classification | |
|---|---|---|---|---|---|
| Travelodge | Travel | Hotel | Avocat | Professional Services | Legal Services |
| Eurostar | Travel | Rail | Avogado | Professional Services | Legal Services |
| Burger | Travel | Subsistence | Law | Professional Services | Legal Services |
| Café | Travel | Subsistence | Lawyer | Professional Services | Legal Services |
| Food | Travel | Subsistence | Legal | Professional Services | Legal Services |
| Pizza | Travel | Subsistence | Solicitor | Professional Services | Legal Services |
| Restaurants | Travel | Subsistence | Bureau Veritas | Professional Services | Testing Services |
| Cabs | Travel | Taxi | Intertek | Professional Services | Testing Services |
| Limo | Travel | Taxi | SGS | Professional Services | Testing Services |
| Lyft | Travel | Taxi | AT&T | Telecoms | Mobile Telecoms |
| Taxi | Travel | Taxi | Bell | Telecoms | Mobile Telecoms |
| Uber | Travel | Taxi | EE | Telecoms | Mobile Telecoms |
| EZ Pass | Travel | Tolls | O2 | Telecoms | Mobile Telecoms |
| E-Z Pass | Travel | Tolls | Telefonica | Telecoms | Mobile Telecoms |
| Toll | Travel | Tolls | Telenor | Telecoms | Mobile Telecoms |
| BCD Travel Travel | Travel | Travel Agents | Telia | Telecoms | Mobile Telecoms |
| Carlson Wagonlit | Travel | Travel Agents | T-Mobile | Telecoms | Mobile Telecoms |
| Dnata | Travel | Travel Agents | Mobile | Telecoms | Telecoms |
| Flight Centre | Travel | Travel Agents | Telecom | Telecoms | Telecoms |

I've suggested the areas that these should be classified under, however, this could be different in your organisation or team, so check these line up with your classification rules. Remember COAT and keep it consistent! And organised, accurate and trustworthy of course! This is also just a sample list of examples; there are many more so remember to scan the data for frequently occurring words or companies.

The next part is VERY important. DO NOT just blindly classify these words or companies with the suggested classifications or your own classifications. It is still essential to look at the context and check the descriptions to make sure it ties in. For example, the word Law could appear as parts of other words, so if you just paste wildly anything with the word Law in the name, you will end up in a world of misclassification pain.

A lot of these words or suppliers might have a single classification, such as a lawyer, taxi or a plumber, and it's great for quickly classifying a lot of rows, but be careful with suppliers like hotels. I'll cover this in more detail when we discuss values, but there is the potential for there to be more than one classification for these suppliers. It's the same with water – it could be utilities or perhaps facilities for watercoolers; and gas can either be utilities or industrial gas depending on which industry you are working in. Be sure to check the full name of the supplier and the description and this will keep you on the right path.

## LLPs

Another potential 'quick win' is around companies that end in LLP. Quite often these are legal or financial professionals, so if you have removed the suffix from the normalised name, perform a search on the original supplier name to find them and then check them alongside the description. Always double-check just to be sure, never assume! You know what they say about assumption . . . it makes an ASS out of U and ME.

You could leave the LLP in the normalised supplier name, but I prefer to remove it so that everything looks cleaner. For me, it's easier to scan the names quickly without the distractions of the LLPs.

## Suppliers with a specific classification

Finally, you will also find that there are some suppliers that will always have a specific classification. I have a list for my team (see below) that we use to make sure they are always classified correctly. Your organisation might differ slightly on the agreement of the classification, but again this is another level of making sure your data has its COAT on and is staying consistent, organised, accurate and trustworthy.

**Table 4.7** *Suppliers with a specific classification*

| Supplier | Classification |
|---|---|
| Avis | Car Hire |
| Budget | Car Hire |
| Dollar | Car Hire |
| Enterprise | Car Hire |

*Continued*

**Table 4.7** *Continued*

| Supplier | Classification |
|---|---|
| Europcar | Car Hire |
| Hertz | Car Hire |
| Sixt | Car Hire |
| ALD | Car Leasing |
| Alphabet | Car Leasing |
| Arval | Car Leasing |
| Leaseplan | Car Leasing |
| Lex Autolease | Car Leasing |
| Canon | Copier Rental |
| Konica Minolta | Copier Rental |
| Ricoh | Copier Rental |
| Xerox | Copier Rental |
| DHL | Courier/Logistics |
| Federal Express | Courier/Logistics |
| TNT | Courier/Logistics |
| UPS | Courier/Logistics |
| Dun & Bradstreet | Credit Checking |
| Equifax | Credit Checking |
| Experian | Credit Checking |
| Shred-IT | Document Destruction |
| Iron Mountain | Document Management |
| Aer Lingus | Flights |
| Air Canada | Flights |
| American Airlines | Flights |
| Delta | Flights |
| Easyjet | Flights |
| Iberia | Flights |
| Ryanair | Flights |
| Southwest Airlines | Flights |
| United Airlines | Flights |
| Francotyp Postalia | Franking machines |
| Neopost/Quadient | Franking machines |
| Pitney Bowes | Franking machines |
| Air Liquide | Industrial Gas |
| BOC | Industrial Gas |
| Linde | Industrial Gas |

*Continued*

| **Table 4.7** *Continued* | |
|---|---|
| CH Robinson | Logistics |
| DB Schenker | Logistics |
| Kuehne & Nagel | Logistics |
| Surveymonkey | Market Research |
| AT&T | Mobile Telecoms |
| Bell | Mobile Telecoms |
| EE | Mobile Telecoms |
| O2 | Mobile Telecoms |
| Telefonica | Mobile Telecoms |
| Telenor | Mobile Telecoms |
| Telia | Mobile Telecoms |
| T-Mobile | Mobile Telecoms |
| Chep | Pallets |
| ADP | Payroll |
| PostNL | Post |
| An Post | Post |
| Canada Post | Post |
| Deutche Post | Post |
| La Poste | Post |
| PostNord | Post |
| Royal Mail | Post & Courier |
| CBRE | Property |
| Jones Lang LaSalle | Property |
| Savills | Property |
| Salesforce | Software |
| Getty Images | Stock Photos |
| Shutterstock | Stock Photos |
| HMRC | Tax |
| Pertemps | Temporary Recruitment |
| Bureau Veritas | Testing Services |
| Intertek | Testing Services |
| SGS | Testing Services |
| Aquaid | Watercoolers |
| Eden Springs | Watercoolers |
| Watercoolers Direct | Watercoolers |
| Waterlogic | Watercoolers |

I recommend that you map this list over the data at the start *and* end of your classification project to make sure it's correct, as we know accidental cut and paste errors, deletions or personal opinions can come into play. You might think that you only need to map it over once at the start and could just remove these suppliers before sending it out for classification. However, there might be an incorrectly normalised version of this supplier that goes out for classification, which gets corrected but is then classified incorrectly and so you end up with multiple classifications against the one supplier. That's why it's good to apply the mapping at the start *and* the end of the classification project to ensure your data keeps its COAT on.

## Deceptive descriptions

Once you've completed these stages, you should have a nice chunk of your rows classified. The next step is to find all the 'quick wins' in the descriptions. Hopefully you've been paying attention and have noticed all the times I've mentioned how important it is to not just look at the description and classify that. Just like when searching through the supplier names, you need to look at the descriptions and supplier name in context. I feel like I may be repeating myself a lot here, but if there's one thing you take from this book, I'd like that to be it.

There are some descriptions where it could only mean one thing, such as a compromise agreement for legal services, but these instances are few and far between so proceed with caution. Then there are other instances where you might have descriptions such as 'taxi from hotel to restaurant' or 'hotel taxi' and you have to be very careful to read the description properly in order to make the right classification.

There are a number of words that I like to call 'deceptive descriptions' and they can have more than one meaning. Watch out for these (Table 4.8).

| Table 4.8 *Examples of deceptive descriptions* | |
|---|---|
| **Asset** | IT, furniture or a building? |
| **Dues** | A subscription or a tax? |
| **Lease** | Property or equipment? |
| **Maintenance** | IT or facilities related? |
| **Rent** | Property or equipment? |
| **Security** | Physical or IT? |
| **Tax** | Business/payroll related or part of a purchase? |

Regardless of all these issues, this is one of my favourite parts of classification. There are so many opportunities to classify a lot of rows quickly and I find it therapeutic and rewarding. Yes, there might be something wrong with me, but someone has to love it!

Here is a list of descriptions, in no particular order, that you might find in your data set along with some suggested classifications:

**Table 4.9** *Examples of descriptions with suggested classifications*

| Word | Classification | | Word | Classification | |
|------|------|------|------|------|------|
| Courier | Facilities | Post & Courier | Caterer | Facilities | Catering |
| Post | Facilities | Post & Courier | Catering | Facilities | Catering |
| Postage | Facilities | Post & Courier | Cleaning | Facilities | Cleaning |
| Floral | HR | Gifts | Limpeza | Facilities | Cleaning |
| Florist | HR | Gifts | Air Con | Facilities | HVAC |
| Flowers | HR | Gifts | HVAC | Facilities | HVAC |
| Gift | HR | Gifts | Furniture | Facilities | Office Furniture |
| Air Ticket | Travel | Air | Ink | Facilities | Office Supplies |
| Flight | Travel | Air | Office Supplies | Facilities | Office Supplies |
| Car Hire | Travel | Car Hire | Stationery | Facilities | Office Supplies |
| Car Rental | Travel | Car Hire | Toner | Facilities | Office Supplies |
| Entertain-ment | Travel | Entertainment | Pest | Facilities | Pest Control |
| Diesel | Travel | Fuel | Pest Control | Facilities | Pest Control |
| Fuel | Travel | Fuel | Lease | Facilities | Rent |
| Petrol | Travel | Fuel | Rent | Facilities | Rent |
| Accom | Travel | Hotel | Extinguisher | Facilities | Security |
| Accommo-dation | Travel | Hotel | Fire | Facilities | Security |
| Hotel | Travel | Hotel | Guard | Facilities | Security |
| Lodging | Travel | Hotel | Security | Facilities | Security |
| Stay | Travel | Hotel | Gas | Facilities | Utilities |
| x nights | Travel | Hotel | Water | Facilities | Utilities |
| Mileage | Travel | Mileage | Placement | HR | Recruitment |
| Car Park | Travel | Parking | Recruitment | HR | Recruitment |
| Parking | Travel | Parking | Temporary | HR | Recruitment |
| Metro | Travel | Rail | Training | HR | Training |
| Oyster | Travel | Rail | Laptop | IT | Computers |

*Continued*

**Table 4.9** *Continued*

| Word | Classification | | Word | Classification | |
|---|---|---|---|---|---|
| Subway | Travel | Rail | Tablet | IT | Computers |
| TFL | Travel | Rail | Keyboard | IT | Peripherals |
| Train | Travel | Rail | Monitor | IT | Peripherals |
| Tube | Travel | Rail | Mouse | IT | Peripherals |
| Underground | Travel | Rail | Webcam | IT | Peripherals |
| Beverage | Travel | Subsistence | License | IT | Software |
| Breakfast | Travel | Subsistence | Software | IT | Software |
| Burger | Travel | Subsistence | Events | Marketing | Event Management |
| Café | Travel | Subsistence | Conference | Marketing | Events |
| Coffee | Travel | Subsistence | Meeting | Marketing | Events |
| Dinner | Travel | Subsistence | Summit | Marketing | Events |
| Food | Travel | Subsistence | Member-ship | Marketing | Memberships |
| GrubHub | Travel | Subsistence | Print | Marketing | Print |
| Lunch | Travel | Subsistence | Translation | Marketing | Translations |
| Meal | Travel | Subsistence | Consultancy | Professional Services | Consulting |
| Pizza | Travel | Subsistence | Consultant | Professional Services | Consulting |
| Refreshment | Travel | Subsistence | Consulting | Professional Services | Consulting |
| Snack | Travel | Subsistence | Accounting | Professional Services | Financial Services |
| Uber Eats | Travel | Subsistence | Audit | Professional Services | Financial Services |
| Addison Lee | Travel | Taxi | Compro-mise Agreement | Professional Services | Legal Services |
| Cab | Travel | Taxi | Legal fees | Professional Services | Legal Services |
| Home to | Travel | Taxi | Legal services | Professional Services | Legal Services |
| Limo | Travel | Taxi | Telephone | Telecoms | Fixed Line |
| Lyft | Travel | Taxi | Telephone | Telecoms | Hardware |
| Taxi | Travel | Taxi | Data | Telecoms | Internet |
| To Home | Travel | Taxi | Internet | Telecoms | Internet |
| Transfer | Travel | Taxi | Wifi | Telecoms | Internet |

*Continued*

**Table 4.9** *Continued*

| Word | Classification | | Word | Classification | |
|------|------|------|------|------|------|
| Uber | Travel | Taxi | EE | Telecoms | Mobile |
| EZ Pass | Travel | Tolls | O2 | Telecoms | Mobile |
| E-Z Pass | Travel | Tolls | Telstra | Telecoms | Mobile |
| Toll | Travel | Tolls | Verizon | Telecoms | Mobile |
| Venue | Travel | Venue Hire | Vodafone | Telecoms | Mobile |
| Visa | Travel | Visa | Cell | Telecoms | Mobile Telecoms |
| Trip | Travel | | Mobile | Telecoms | Mobile Telecoms |
| Visit | Travel | | Telecom | Telecoms | Telecoms |
| Meeting with | Travel | | Watercooler | Facilities | Watercoolers |

### Typos and abbreviations

Within the description columns, you will always find typos and abbreviations. They might be specific to your business or industry and you may or may not be familiar with them. If you scan the data you should be able to pick up on the frequent ones. Some great examples of typos I've seen include the ones below (you have to be a mind reader to figure out what is going on sometimes)!

**Table 4.10** *Common typos*

| | | |
|------|------|------|
| Mileage | Carriage | Travel |
| Mileeage | Carrugae | Trvael |
| Milegae | Carrige | Trval |
| Milegage | Carraige | Trvale |
| Milege | Carrage | Trvaling |
| Milelage | | Trvel |
| Trainning Milage | | |

My spell checker went mad with these, as well as with the abbreviations overleaf, which you'll commonly find in the MRO world. (Especially the o-ring – I've seen that spelt so many different ways and just when you think you've found them all, another one appears! Table 4.11 on the next page).

While the above might not be relevant to your industry, it will give you an idea of what you should be looking out for in your own data sets and get you thinking about how certain things might be abbreviated.

Once you've exhausted all your avenues with quick wins, you'll still be left with a number of rows. Some of the descriptions could be very vague, such as 'services', 'delivery' or 'items', which on their own are hard to classify, but in context might mean something else. This is where looking at what you have classified so far could help you classify more rows quickly.

**Table 4.11** *Common abbreviations in MRO*

| Name | Abbreviations | | |
|---|---|---|---|
| Bearing | Brg | | |
| Bolts | Blt | Blts | |
| Coupling | Cplg | | |
| Filters | Fltr | Fltrs | |
| Gasket | Gskt | | |
| Holder | Hldr | | |
| Lubricant | Lube | Lubrtg | Lubrct |
| O-Rings | O-Ring | Oring | O Ring |
| Roller | Rlr | | |
| Safety | Sfty | | |
| Screws | Scrw | Scr | Scws |
| Shackle | Shkl | | |
| Valve | Vlv | | |
| Washer | Wshr | | |
| Wheel | Whl | | |

## Partially classified suppliers

This next step will only work well and be time-efficient if you have a small amount of data. With the full set of the data, classified and unclassified, create a new pivot in the usual format: tabular form, no totals or subtotals and repeat all item labels, with normalised name and the classification columns. Untick the blanks from the normalised supplier column (if any) and collapse field from the PivotTable Analyze tab (Figure 4.1 opposite).

In this format, you can scroll down the suppliers and look for where there are only two classifications – one from the taxonomy and one (blank). By setting up your view as New Window and Arrange All > Horizontally with side-by-side tabs, as shown in Chapters 1 and 2, you can have the pivot tab and the raw data tab, and you can go through and update the data as you find them, remembering to hit that Refresh All button in the data tab on your pivot tab of course.

From there on in, all that's left is blood, sweat and tears to classify the data. There might be lots or there might be none, but I can guarantee it's all the fiddly bits that are left to classify and this will be the most time-consuming part of the job. It will probably be the part that takes up 80%

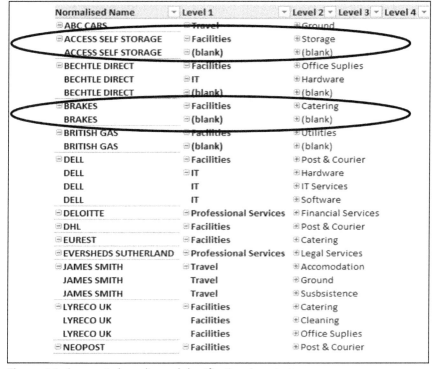

| Normalised Name | Level 1 | Level 2 | Level 3 | Level 4 |
|---|---|---|---|---|
| ABC CABS | Travel | Ground | | |
| ACCESS SELF STORAGE | Facilities | Storage | | |
| ACCESS SELF STORAGE | (blank) | (blank) | | |
| BECHTLE DIRECT | Facilities | Office Suplies | | |
| BECHTLE DIRECT | IT | Hardware | | |
| BECHTLE DIRECT | (blank) | (blank) | | |
| BRAKES | Facilities | Catering | | |
| BRAKES | (blank) | (blank) | | |
| BRITISH GAS | Facilities | Utilities | | |
| BRITISH GAS | (blank) | (blank) | | |
| DELL | Facilities | Post & Courier | | |
| DELL | IT | Hardware | | |
| DELL | IT | IT Services | | |
| DELL | IT | Software | | |
| DELOITTE | Professional Services | Financial Services | | |
| DHL | Facilities | Post & Courier | | |
| EUREST | Facilities | Catering | | |
| EVERSHEDS SUTHERLAND | Professional Services | Legal Services | | |
| JAMES SMITH | Travel | Accomodation | | |
| JAMES SMITH | Travel | Ground | | |
| JAMES SMITH | Travel | Susbsistence | | |
| LYRECO UK | Facilities | Catering | | |
| LYRECO UK | Facilities | Cleaning | | |
| LYRECO UK | Facilities | Office Suplies | | |
| NEOPOST | Facilities | Post & Courier | | |

**Figure 4.1** *Aggregated supplier and classifications in a pivot*

of your time for the whole project. The good news is that once you've done it, you're lightening the load for future data refreshes.

## Tricky suppliers

We haven't spoken about how to find those tricky suppliers yet, the ones that have a vague or generic name, don't have a good description, are quite possibly in another country and most likely in another language.

Some of my favourites include suppliers like 1234567 Ontario Inc, John Smith or those with a common business name such as Swift or Four Seasons (is it a hotel or a landscaping company?). This is where Google searching comes in. Yes, there are other search engines available, however, I have found they do not deliver the same level of accuracy in results as Google. The choice is yours though and the process should still work regardless of which one you choose.

The questions to think about when you have tricky suppliers are: (a) is there a suffix in the original supplier name; (b) do I know what country they are based in; and (c) do I have any information from the invoice description that is useful? If the answer to these questions is 'no', all is not lost; you might still be able to get the country information from your business that you can map into the data. If all else fails, send an e-mail round to all of the category managers to see if they know who the supplier is.

Let's start by searching by the original supplier name. The suffix can tell you a lot about where a company is based, for example, Inc will most likely be the USA, GMBH is usually Germany, OY is the Nordics, S.A. is Spain or Portugal, SP ZOO is usually Poland, B.V. or N.V. the Netherlands or sometimes Belgium, and Limited or Ltd tends to be the UK.

If you search for Company 123 Inc, you might get taken straight to the right website. Result! But a word of caution: just like classification, when searching it's always important to ask 'would the company I'm classifying for use this product or service?' If the answer is 'yes' then great, you've found your classification and can move on. If it's a 'no', the first thing I would try is searching with quote marks, i.e. 'Company 123 Inc'. If this still doesn't return any results, look to see if you have any useable descriptions that might be useful for searching, such as food, tools or maintenance. Even words like 'services' can help to guide you. Try running a search on 'Company 123 Inc food' with or without quote marks, and if that fails, try 'Company 123 Inc food USA' - you never know!

Sometimes you just can't find certain companies. I've gone back to my clients with a list and even they have struggled to find out who the supplier is and what they do, so don't be disappointed if you can't find them all.

Once you've exhausted the suppliers with suffixes, it's time to work on any that have country and description information. If you start with the country information, this is more important and more likely to guide you in the right direction. If you search on description first, you could have a company in your own country providing something similar and end up with the wrong classification.

The thing to remember about using search engines is that you are automatically directed to the home page of the country you are in. If you are only searching companies within your location, that's fine, but if you are working with multiple countries you need to be aware of this when carrying out your search. If you only have suppliers from one other country, you can go to the country home page of that search engine and run your searches from there, however, if there's one other country in your data set, there's likely to be lots of other countries too.

To give an example, we know that Company ABC is from Sweden because there was a country column in our data. The first thing to do is try searching Company ABC Sweden. Hopefully this should return your result. If not, try 'Company ABC Sweden'. If this fails, try 'Company ABC

Sweden and [description]' if you have it. If you don't have a description, fear not, it's not the end of the road yet.

The next step is to try searching 'Company ABC Sweden [company I'm classifying for]'. This can deliver results, not often, but it can help. If there's been any press around a collaboration between the two companies then you might be able to find it. If you can't find it after this stage, I would either use the GL code as a very last resort or, if that doesn't make any sense, I would hand it back to the client for further information. If it's a person's name, I would classify it under consultancy if the value was low, say under £20k. Plus, you know where to find the supplier if it needs to be changed.

The last combination to try if you don't have a suffix or the country information is to search by description only. Again, you would start with Company ABC [description] and see if you can find it from there. If that fails, try with 'Company ABC [description]', and if that fails, try 'Company ABC [description] [company I'm classifying for]'. You can try with or without the description to see if you get better results. Basically, anything you can try – do it! Again, if all those avenues have failed to help you find what the supplier does, your back-up option is the GL code.

There's one bonus tip for you, which is more like a shot in the dark, but again it can deliver results. If you suspect you know the country where the company is, for example, you're working on a UK file, then you can add 'Limited' or 'Ltd' to the end of the company name and you might just get a result.

That's exactly how I found that the Tinder Corporation in my client's file was not *the* Tinder that you swipe left on. Again, this is where context comes into play. The client was a UK-based charity and I just knew there was no way they were paying a business subscription to the dating app. I took a chance and searched for Tinder Corporation Ltd and it came up as a UK company listed on the Companies House website, the official registry of companies in the UK. Bingo!

When you start working with your own data, you'll find tips and tricks specific to your company and data that you can use, but these search methods I have shared with you have not failed me yet. I know that if I can't find the company via this method, the chances are I won't find it at all.

## Updating new data with existing classified data

When you have your fully classified data file, there are two steps to semi-automate classification in future data refreshes. The first is to map over suppliers with a single classification by normalised name only using a

VLOOKUP; the other is to map over on a combination of the supplier name and the description for exact matches using the CONCATENATE and VLOOKUP functions.

I would always complete these tasks in the order that I've just listed them. Why? If you know a supplier should only have a single classification, it doesn't matter what the description is, you don't need to match on that. You are saving time and effort by applying this step first, it will leave you with less data to map at the second stage and then again at the final manual classification step.

The first thing to do is to create your master files. Let's start with the Supplier Classification Master. With a fully classified set of data – and I can't emphasise enough, you have to have all the suppliers and descriptions classified (so that you don't classify the new data with the word (blanks)) – create a pivot table. You know the drill now: tabular form, no totals or subtotals and repeat all item labels, with normalised name and the classification columns. Untick the blanks from the normalise supplier column (if any) and collapse field from the PivotTable Analyze tab.

Next, copy the whole table of normalised supplier names and their classification and paste as values, either to the right of the pivot table or in a new tab. Wherever you paste it, make sure there is a blank column to the left of the table.

This will now be a list of all the suppliers and their classifications. The aim is to find all single classification suppliers from that list, which we will do with a COUNTIF formula in the blank column to the left (Figure 4.2 opposite).

You want to find the number of times each supplier name appears. With the COUNTIF formula, select the column that the normalised supplier name is in, in this case column I, and if it's a range, fix this with $ around the column letter.

Finally, you want to double-check that it's the normalised supplier name that's on the same row as the formula that's been selected and not a different row (Figure 4.3). Copy the formula down, then perform a couple of spot checks to make sure that the numbers add up correctly. When you're confident that they do, filter on the 1s and this will give you a list of all your normalised suppliers with a unique classification (Figure 4.4 on the next page).

Copy this into a new Excel file and name it something descriptive that says what it is, like 'Supplier Classification Master'. Name the tab within it 'raw data' and you can then copy this into the refresh data whenever needed. When your refresh data is ready, copy that tab over into the refresh

| | Normalised Name | Level 1 | Level 2 | Level 3 | Level 4 |
|---|---|---|---|---|---|
| =COUNTIF($I$4:$I$39,I4) | | Travel | Ground | Taxi | |
| | ACCESS SELF STORAGE | Facilities | Storage | Self Storage | |
| | BECHTLE DIRECT | Facilities | Office Suplies | | |
| | BECHTLE DIRECT | IT | Hardware | Accessories | |
| | BECHTLE DIRECT | IT | Hardware | Tablets | |
| | BECHTLE DIRECT | IT | Hardware | Tablets | |
| | BRAKES | Facilities | Catering | Food & Drink | |
| | BRITISH GAS | Facilities | Utilities | | |
| | BRITISH GAS | Facilities | Utilities | Electricity | |
| | DELL | IT | Hardware | Computers | |
| | DELL | IT | Hardware | Peripherals | |
| | DELL | IT | Hardware | Servers | |

**Figure 4.2**  *COUNTIF formula*

file, always preserving the original master copy, and using a VLOOKUP, pull through the classification levels (Figure 4.5, page 93).

When you've copied the formula down, it should look something like this (Figure 4.6), unless you are really lucky and match on most suppliers. For the rest of us, we are grateful for the matches we do find as that has

| | Normalised Name | Level 1 | Level 2 | Level 3 | Level 4 |
|---|---|---|---|---|---|
| 1 | ABC CARS | Travel | Ground | Taxi | |
| 1 | ACCESS SELF STORAGE | Facilities | Storage | Self Storage | |
| 3 | BECHTLE DIRECT | Facilities | Office Suplies | | |
| 3 | BECHTLE DIRECT | IT | Hardware | Accessories | |
| 3 | BECHTLE DIRECT | IT | Hardware | Tablets | |
| 1 | BECHTLE DIRECT | IT | Hardware | Tablets | |
| 1 | BRAKES | Facilities | Catering | Food & Drink | |
| 2 | BRITISH GAS | Facilities | Utilities | | |
| 2 | BRITISH GAS | Facilities | Utilities | Electricity | |
| 6 | DELL | IT | Hardware | Computers | |
| 6 | DELL | IT | Hardware | Peripherals | |
| 6 | DELL | IT | Hardware | Servers | |
| 6 | DELL | IT | Hardware | (blank) | |
| 6 | DELL | IT | IT Services | | |
| 6 | DELL | IT | Software | | |
| 1 | DELOITTE | Professional Services | Financial Services | Audit | |
| 1 | DHL | Facilities | Post & Courier | Courier | |
| 2 | EUREST | Facilities | Catering | Catering Services | |
| 2 | EUREST | Facilities | Catering | Food & Drink | |
| 1 | EVERSHEDS SUTHERLAND | Professional Services | Legal Services | | |
| 3 | JAMES SMITH | Travel | Accomodation | Hotel | |
| 3 | JAMES SMITH | Travel | Ground | Taxi | |
| 3 | JAMES SMITH | Travel | Susbsistence | | |
| 5 | LYRECO UK | Facilities | Catering | Food & Drink | |
| 5 | LYRECO UK | Facilities | Cleaning | Cleaning Supplies | |
| 5 | LYRECO UK | Facilities | Office Suplies | Mailing Supplies | |
| 5 | LYRECO UK | Facilities | Office Suplies | Office Furniture | |
| 5 | LYRECO UK | Facilities | Office Suplies | Office Machines | |

**Figure 4.3**  *Results of copying the formula down*

| Normalised Name | Level 1 | Level 2 | Level 3 | Level 4 |
|---|---|---|---|---|
| 1 ABC CARS | Travel | Ground | Taxi | |
| 1 ACCESS SELF STORAGE | Facilities | Storage | Self Storage | |
| 1 BECHTLE DIRECT | IT | Hardware | Tablets | |
| 1 BRAKES | Facilities | Catering | Food & Drink | |
| 1 DELOITTE | Professional Services | Financial Services | Audit | |
| 1 DHL | Facilities | Post & Courier | Courier | |
| 1 EVERSHEDS SUTHERLAND | Professional Services | Legal Services | | |
| 1 NEOPOST | Facilities | Post & Courier | Franking Machines | |
| 1 TELE TAXIS | Travel | Ground | Taxi | |
| 1 UBER | Travel | Ground | Taxi | |
| 1 XYZ SOLICITORS | Professional Services | Legal Services | | |

**Figure 4.4** *Filtering on unique classifications*

just saved us potentially hours or days of classification. This also helps our data keep its COAT on. It's a win-win situation.

It's really important at this stage to change the formulas to values before we do anything else.  Select and highlight the column headers where the formulas are and right-click>copy, then paste special>values.

The next task is to go through and cleanse the data, deleting any N/As or 0s. The safest way to do this is to filter on the N/As, 0s or anything else that's not a classification and delete them. You could also apply a search and replace on the selected columns, but if you have these specific letters or numbers in your taxonomy it could remove them. Even worse, if you forget to select the classification columns, you could end up doing a search and replace on the whole file, which you might not immediately notice and would be disastrous.

## Mapping classifications using CONCATENATE and VLOOKUP

Once the data has been tidied up, we can move on to mapping classifications that match on normalised supplier name and description using CONCATENATE and VLOOKUP.

Firstly, we have to create a unique list of normalised supplier names and descriptions to map into the refresh data. Unlike the supplier name by classification, you should have a unique list just by creating a pivot with the normalised supplier name, description and classification columns. If you have a large amount of data, you might have multiple classifications

|  | B | C | D | E | F |
|---|---|---|---|---|---|
|  | Normalised Name | Description | Level 1 | Level 2 | Level 3 |
|  | ABC CARS | Taxi | =VLOOKUP(B2,'Raw data'!$A:$E,2,0) | =VLOOKUP(B2,'Raw data'!$A:$E,3,0) | =VLOOKUP(B2,'Raw data'!$A:$E,4,0) |
|  | ABC CARS | Pickup |  |  |  |

**Figure 4.5** *VLOOKUP for updating new data with existing classified data*

|  | B | C | D | E | F | G |  |
|---|---|---|---|---|---|---|---|
|  | Normalised Name | Description | Level 1 | Level 2 | Level 3 | Level 4 |  |
|  | ABC CARS | Taxi | Travel | Ground | Taxi |  | 0 |
|  | ABC CARS | Pickup | Travel | Ground | Taxi |  | 0 |
|  | ACCESS SELF STORAGE | Storage Costs | Facilities | Storage | Self Storage |  | 0 |
|  | ACCESS SELF STORAGE | Storage Costs | Facilities | Storage | Self Storage |  | 0 |
|  | ACCESS SELF STORAGE | Storage Costs | Facilities | Storage | Self Storage |  | 0 |
|  | ACCESS SELF STORAGE | Storage Costs | Facilities | Storage | Self Storage |  | 0 |
|  | ACCESS SELF STORAGE | Storage Costs | Facilities | Storage | Self Storage |  | 0 |
|  | ACCESS SELF STORAGE | Storage Costs | Facilities | Storage | Self Storage |  | 0 |
|  | ACCESS SELF STORAGE | Storage Costs | Facilities | Storage | Self Storage |  | 0 |
|  | ACCESS SELF STORAGE | Storage Costs | Facilities | Storage | Self Storage |  | 0 |
|  | BECHTLE DIRECT | County Adhesive Tape | #N/A | #N/A | #N/A | #N/A | 0 |
|  | BECHTLE DIRECT | Office Stationery | #N/A | #N/A | #N/A | #N/A | 0 |
|  | BECHTLE DIRECT | 2m HDMI V2.0 4K UHD | #N/A | #N/A | #N/A | #N/A | 0 |
|  | BECHTLE DIRECT | 5m VGA Monitor Conn | #N/A | #N/A | #N/A | #N/A | 0 |
|  | BECHTLE DIRECT | Apple Pencil iPad Pro . | #N/A | #N/A | #N/A | #N/A | 0 |
|  | BECHTLE DIRECT | Apple Pencil iPad Pro iT |  | Hardware | Tablets |  | 0 |
|  | BECHTLE DIRECT | 5m VGA Monitor Conn | #N/A | #N/A | #N/A | #N/A | 0 |
|  | BECHTLE DIRECT | 2m HDMI V2.0 4K UHD | #N/A | #N/A | #N/A | #N/A | 0 |
|  | BECHTLE DIRECT | Office Stationery | #N/A | #N/A | #N/A | #N/A | 0 |
|  | BECHTLE DIRECT | County Adhesive Tape | #N/A | #N/A | #N/A | #N/A | 0 |
|  | BRAKES | Apples | Facilities | Catering | Food & Drink |  | 0 |
|  | BRAKES | Bananas | Facilities | Catering | Food & Drink |  | 0 |
|  | BRAKES | Oranges | Facilities | Catering | Food & Drink |  | 0 |

**Figure 4.6** *How the data should look with VLOOKUP applied*

against a unique combination of a supplier and description. If you want to be sure this is not the case, you could repeat the COUNTIF step that was used for the unique supplier classifications.

Next, copy this table into a new spreadsheet, naming it something meaningful like 'Supplier Description Classification Master', leaving a blank column to the left of the data. In that blank column, use the CONCATENATE formula to append the normalised name and description (Figure 4.7 opposite). You don't need to worry about including a space, you just need a unique lookup to match on in the refresh file.

Apply that formula to all the rows and double-check it has worked properly throughout the data (Figure 4.8). You don't *have* to do this next step, but I recommend it as Excel can be very sensitive when it comes to formulas and lookups. Copy the column, which I've named 'Lookup', and right click>paste special>values or the VLOOKUP used later in the process might not work.

For the next step you can take two approaches. The first is to map this list directly into the existing data, which is partially classified already. Just filter on the blank values and apply the formulas to that. This is the quickest method but is open to errors if you accidentally override the existing classified data.

The alternative approach is to copy the unclassified data into a new tab, use the formulas to pull through the data, and then pull that data through to the original file using a VLOOKUP. I would only choose this option if you are really concerned about the integrity of the data.

I'll be using the first option as an example. As long as you are careful, it should be okay, but always make sure you have a back-up copy just in case.

Firstly, we need a lookup column in our refresh data. You may or may not know this, but the reason that the lookup columns are on the left is that they need to come first in order for the lookup to work. Insert a new column to the left of the supplier columns and repeat the CONCATENATE step from above in this file. The CONCATENATE formula has to be exactly the same or the VLOOKUP won't work later in the process.

I'd recommend pasting the lookup formula as values, then, as with the earlier step where we used the VLOOKUP to pull through the classification on the normalised name, add a VLOOKUP to the first classification column (Figure 4.9, page 96). In this instance, make sure you fix the lookup cell with a $ and remember to increase the column number by one for each level of the classification.

When you're confident that the first row of formulas is correct, you MUST drag the formula down (Figure 4.10). This is because you have a filter on and, if you cut and paste, it will potentially overwrite other data

| Lookup | Normalised Name | Description | Level 1 | Level 2 | Level 3 | Level 4 |
|---|---|---|---|---|---|---|
| =CONCATENATE(B2,C2) | | Pickup | Travel | Ground | Taxi | |
| CONCATENATE(text1, [text2], [text3] ...) | | Taxi | Travel | Ground | Taxi | |
| | ACCESS SELF STORAGE | Storage Costs | Facilities | Storage | Self Storage | |

**Figure 4.7**  *Applying a CONCATENATE formula*

| Lookup | Normalised Name | Description | Level 1 | Level 2 | Level 3 | Level 4 |
|---|---|---|---|---|---|---|
| ABC CARSPickup | ABC CARS | Pickup | Travel | Ground | Taxi | |
| ABC CARSTaxi | ABC CARS | Taxi | Travel | Ground | Taxi | |
| ACCESS SELF STORAGEStorage Costs | ACCESS SELF STORAGE | Storage Costs | Facilities | Storage | Self Storage | |
| BECHTLE DIRECT2m HDMI V2.0 4K UHD Connector Cable | BECHTLE DIRECT | 2m HDMI V2.0 4K UHD Connector Cable | IT | Hardware | Accessories | |
| BECHTLE DIRECT5m VGA Monitor Connector Cable | BECHTLE DIRECT | 5m VGA Monitor Connector Cable | IT | Hardware | Accessories | |
| BECHTLE DIRECTApple Pencil iPad Pro 2. Gen Pen | BECHTLE DIRECT | Apple Pencil iPad Pro 2. Gen Pen | IT | Hardware | Tablets | |
| BECHTLE DIRECTCounty Adhesive Tape - Printed Fragile | BECHTLE DIRECT | County Adhesive Tape - Printed Fragile | Facilities | Office Suplies | | |
| BECHTLE DIRECTOffice Stationery | BECHTLE DIRECT | Office Stationery | Facilities | Office Suplies | | |
| BECHTLE DIRECT Apple Pencil iPad Pro 2. Gen Pen | BECHTLE DIRECT | Apple Pencil iPad Pro 2. Gen Pen | IT | Hardware | Tablets | |
| BRAKESApples | BRAKES | Apples | Facilities | Catering | Food & Drink | |
| BRAKESBananas | BRAKES | Bananas | Facilities | Catering | Food & Drink | |
| BRAKESBeef | BRAKES | Beef | Facilities | Catering | Food & Drink | |
| BRAKESBeverages | BRAKES | Beverages | Facilities | Catering | Food & Drink | |
| BRAKESBread | BRAKES | Bread | Facilities | Catering | Food & Drink | |
| BRAKESChicken | BRAKES | Chicken | Facilities | Catering | Food & Drink | |
| BRAKESMeals | BRAKES | Meals | Facilities | Catering | Food & Drink | |
| BRAKESMilk | BRAKES | Milk | Facilities | Catering | Food & Drink | |
| BRAKESOranges | BRAKES | Oranges | Facilities | Catering | Food & Drink | |
| BRAKESPork | BRAKES | Pork | Facilities | Catering | Food & Drink | |
| BRITISH GAS01/01-31/03 charges | BRITISH GAS | 01/01-31/03 charges | Facilities | Utilities | | |

**Figure 4.8**  *How the data should look when the CONCATENATE formula is applied*

| | A | B | C | D | E |
|---|---|---|---|---|---|
| | Lookup | Supplier Nam | Normalised Nar | Description | Level 1 |
| | BECHTLE DIRECTCounty Adhesive Tape | Bechtle Direct L | BECHTLE DIRECT | County Adhesive Tape - Printed Fragile | =VLOOKUP($A12,'Supplier description lookup'!$A:$G,4,0) |
| | BECHTLE DIRECTOffice Stationery | Bechtle Direct L | BECHTLE DIRECT | Office Stationery | |

**Figure 4.9** *Using a VLOOKUP on the concatenated data*

| B | C | D | E | F | G | H |
|---|---|---|---|---|---|---|
| Supplier Nam | Normalised Nar | Description | Level 1 | Level 2 | Level 3 | Level 4 |
| Bechtle Direct L | BECHTLE DIRECT | County Adhesive Tape - Printed Fragile | Facilities | Office Suplies | | 0 |
| Bechtle Direct L | BECHTLE DIRECT | Office Stationery | Facilities | Office Suplies | | 0 |
| Bechtle Direct L | BECHTLE DIRECT | 2m HDMI V2.0 4K UHD Connector Cable | IT | Hardware | Accessories | 0 |
| Bechtle Direct L | BECHTLE DIRECT | 5m VGA Monitor Connector Cable | IT | Hardware | Accessories | 0 |
| Bechtle Direct L | BECHTLE DIRECT | Apple Pencil iPad Pro 2. Gen Pen | IT | Hardware | Tablets | 0 |
| Bechtle Direct L | BECHTLE DIRECT | Apple Pencil iPad Pro 2. Gen Pen | IT | Hardware | Tablets | 0 |
| Bechtle Direct L | BECHTLE DIRECT | 5m VGA Monitor Connector Cable | IT | Hardware | Accessories | 0 |
| Bechtle Direct L | BECHTLE DIRECT | 2m HDMI V2.0 4K UHD Connector Cable | IT | Hardware | Accessories | 0 |
| Bechtle Direct L | BECHTLE DIRECT | Office Stationery | Facilities | Office Suplies | | 0 |

**Figure 4.10** *How the VLOOKUP data should look*

hidden in the filter. Once you've done this and have completed some spot checks to make sure the classification looks accurate, take the filter off, highlight those classification columns, copy and then paste as values.

## Refreshing the data

After tidying up the N/As and 0s, whatever you have left is ready to manually classify. When you first start this, you might find you don't get many matches from the existing data. However, each time you refresh your data, you are building bigger master data files, so in theory every time you run this exercise, you should have less left to manually classify.

At the end of each refresh, you'll need to update each of your master files with new suppliers and supplier/descriptions. The most efficient way to do this is as follows: for the master supplier classification by name, create a pivot of the normalised supplier name and classification, then use the COUNTIF function to find the unique classifications.

Add this list to your existing master file, then create a pivot to get a unique list of classifications. At this point, they *should* be unique, but you can either scroll down to check the names in the pivot table or do a COUNTIF formula to double-check. Remember, you can't have trustworthy data without it being consistent, organised and accurate!

If you do have any conflicting classifications, review which one is the most suitable option and remember to update any existing data with the changes you have made. Copy and save this list. It will now become the Supplier Classification Master and override any previous versions.

Next, you need to apply the same process to the supplier name and description master. Create a pivot from the refresh data and check to make sure they are unique either by scrolling through or using the COUNTIF function. Add these to the master file and then create a new pivot to make sure they are all unique classifications. Again, if you do have any multiple classifications against a unique combination of the supplier name and description, choose the most suitable option and remember to update any existing data.

When you are happy this is correct, make this the Supplier Description Classification Master, or whatever you want to call it - but remember that the filename has to work for you and your team.

## Conclusion

We have covered *a lot* in this chapter: best practice, how to classify, how to update refreshes, creating and updating master classification files - the list goes on. The most important takeaway is this: *context is everything; without it data gets misclassified.* Use as much of the data as a whole as you can, looking at supplier name, description and values. Within that context, you need to think about 'who am I classifying for?' and 'would this company buy this product or service?'

When you're classifying, keep the COAT on in your approach. Make sure you and your team classify suppliers or descriptions to the same category. Keep them consistent and that will ensure they're organised, which in turn will make your data accurate and therefore trustworthy. Agree these standards amongst your team beforehand and draw up a list. I've provided you with some to get started, but customise it to the needs of your business.

Apply your checks with pivot tables, as I've shown you, and you will have a great master file, ready to update your data at the next refresh. This will save you not only time but also potential classification errors.

And don't forget to watch out for those typos!!

# 5 Basic Data Cleansing

## Cleansing personal data

We have focused a lot on classification and normalisation, but what about other data cleansing such as supplier or customer addresses? I have seen first hand how many duplicates can occur if you're working with multiple systems.

I had a client with nine different sources of data, which when merged totalled 2.8 million rows of customer information. When I cleansed this, it reduced to 1.3 million rows of data. I certainly didn't do this in Excel, and there are a number of tools available that can help, but if you're on a budget or need to get something done relatively quickly, I can show you how to achieve this using Excel.

It would be hard to cover all the different formats that addresses can come in. Quite often you will see a mixture of formats, such as everything in one cell or spread across many cells or with the information in the wrong column. I'll be focusing on names, addresses and e-mails for this exercise, but you will most likely have telephone numbers as well.

I'll share as an example what I'm going to call my sample customer list (Figure 5.1 on the next page). It's got a name and address and an e-mail column and there is a mixture of upper and lower case data, as well as sentence case. This is not unusual and I see this in a lot of files. Again, it's down to creating some standards and making sure everyone applies them.

As all the formulas used for this process are in previous chapters, there will be less illustrations in this chapter, but feel free to refer back to Chapters 1, 2 and 4 if you'd like some visual support.

## Cleansing names in Excel

There are a number of different ways to approach this and it very much depends on what you need for your business. In my sample file, the names are all in one column. Is that how you want them to stay? Or do you want to split them out into first name and last name? This is most likely something that is decided elsewhere in the business, but it doesn't mean you can't use their standards and formatting and be consistent. Yes, COAT still applies here!

| Name | Address | New email |
|---|---|---|
| 104 Deanhill Court | 104 Deanhill Court | jkl@live.co.uk |
| 13 Pallatina | First place Walsall Ws64jh | namefirst@hotmail.com |
| 14 . | Heol Isaf | lastneamefirstname@hotmail.com |
| 17 oxford street | 17 oxford Lane barrow in furness cumbria LA14 7JA | proseccoqueen@hotmail.co.uk |
| 18 . | hop bine close eastpeckham,tonbridge kent TN127JN | ihateexcel@hotmail.com |
| 235 . | AYR drive | jkl@hotmail.com |
| 24 . | Mendip drive  HORNCHURCH Essex RM11 1LL | boozy@btinternet.com |
| 35 . | Heritage drive  Chatham Kent ME77SQ | queenofprosecco@hotmail.co.uk |
|  | 42 Primrose way Thornbury Bristol BS47 1UA | light@hotmail.com |
| 61 Devereux | Cresent Stroud Glos GL74PX | lastneamefirstname@hotmail.co.uk |
| 7 . | Holly Bank | dopey@hotmail.co.uk |
| 70 . | Beacon Ave | janedoe@hotmail.com |
| 71 Collins | Henryville Meadows Ballyclare BT400FY | Robbie@sky.com |
| 75 . | 77 Wells drive | jimjams@hotmail.com |
| 83 south parade | Colin Sykes Foodstores | tents@live.co.uk |
| Andy azim | 12 Rokesby drive  Slough SL2 2EA | 234@gmail.com |
| Andy Bull | 14 Jubilee Close | clean.data@hotmail.com |
| Andy dengel | 24 Mossbank place LUTON LU2 0HH | first.last@gmail.com |
| Andy ONeil | 10 Chapel Lane West Bromwich B700ST | abc@gmail.com |
| Beth aaassss | 4 Elm Grove drive  London W74JH | dopey@yahoo.co.uk |
| Beth Ahmed | 10 the coppice Cheshire Wa17 0du | TomA@hotmail.co.uk |

**Figure 5.1**  *Sample of personal data*

It's the same with the addresses. Do you want the address all in one column or do you need it split into address 1, 2, 3, 4 and then town or city and postcode? Make a decision and be consistent in it. Again, you might have to work to the rules of the business, but that's fine as long as everything is the same.

You might think a quick way to check for duplicates in Excel is conditional formatting on the name, for example. You can then scroll down to look for duplicates or filter on the colour. However, a problem occurs when you have the same name, but different postal or e-mail addresses. This gives a false positive as some of those records are not duplicates, they are legitimately there.

## Splitting first name and last name

I generally see that the names of individuals are split out into First Name and Last Name, and that's the task we'll deal with first. Copy the Name column into a new tab in the spreadsheet. Next, create a second copy of this column right next to the first. The reason for this is that you need the first column as a lookup later on in the process.

Highlight the second column that you pasted the name into (or column B if you started pasting from column A) and, on the ribbon at the top, go to the Data tab. Select Text to Columns, choose the delimited option and then click next. You may or may not be familiar with Text to Columns so I'll talk you through it in case this is new to you.

In the next box, you'll be faced with a number of options. How your original data is formatted will determine the selection you choose. In this case, we want to separate the first name and last name using a space as that is how it is separated in the original data. (In a different data set it could be a different character such as a full stop or a comma.)

Click next again, select General for Column data format and click Finish. You'll see that wherever there is a space between names, this word has been separated out. For the majority of your data this will be great, however, there will be some names that are split out into three or even four columns, so we need to go through and tidy these up.

I'm going to start by renaming the second column First Name and the one after, Last Name or Surname. A great way to find those extra long names that need to be put back together is by adding a filter to the whole row so you can see how many columns have data in there.

With my names spread out into four columns, I'm going to go to the furthest away column and I'm going to deselect the blank columns. This leaves me with three names I need to merge into two columns. Now three names is not a lot and I could just manually correct these (remember what I said about not over-engineering the process?), but you'll find as you move closer to the original data, each column will have more names. That's when you'll need our good friend the CONCATENATE formula (Figure 5.2 opposite). Once I've manually corrected that first end column, I move into the next one along to my left and filter out the blanks, which reveals that it does have a lot more names. Further along in a blank column, start your CONCATENATE formula. I like to use the box to help with this as it shows what the output will be from the formula before I hit OK. This is very handy if the output that you're looking for is wrong!

As you can see, it's the middle initial that's causing the problem. I want to concatenate this and the first name together, but I need to make sure there is a space in-between the two words. In the formula, I use " " to make sure that the space is recognised. In this example (Figure 5.2), I can see that the output is Bill C - exactly what I want.

I've double-clicked to drag down the formula, not to copy it as there's a filter on (lessons learned from previous chapters). Next, I need to copy that information into the First Name column, but of course it's not that easy because there are filters on. Plus, it's a formula and I'm about to use another formula so it may not pull through without values.

The best thing to do here is to clear the filter in the CONCATENATE formula column, then copy that whole column and paste special>values. Then, put that filter back on where there are values, as the next thing to do is pull through the concatenated name to the First Name column, either by cut and paste if it's a small number of names or by an =(the cell that the concatenated name is in). If you look at the example above, it would be Column E.

Next, double-click the green square in the corner to copy that formula down, check that the new names (including the initials) are now in the First Name column, reset the filter, copy the First Name column and paste special>values. It is really important that after each step you remove any formulas as that's when mistakes can happen.

We now need to move the last name into the Last Name column. You'll need to put that original concatenate column back on to a filter with values only (column E in the example above) and use the formula =(cell that the last name is in). In this instance you are putting the formula into column C, pulling through the name from column D. You might want to delete the data in column C first, but that's a personal preference. Copy in the usual way by double-clicking or dragging, never copy and paste, and then clear the filters, copy the Last Name column and paste special>values.

Once that's done, make sure you clear any formula columns before you

| B | C | D |
|---|---|---|
| First Name | Last Name | |
| | 104 Deanhill | Court |
| | 17 oxford | street |
| | 83 south | parade |
| Bill | C | Crowe |
| Bill | C | King |
| Bill | L | Pollock |
| Bill | m | Claydon |
| Bill | m | Claydon |
| Bill | m | Claydon |
| Chanel | d | firth |
| Chanel | d | firth |
| Dave | J | Thomson |
| David | aaazz | zzzaaa |
| David | l | rowlands |
| David | R | SWANSON |
| David | R | SWANSON |
| Derek | T | JESS |
| Eric | L | Minogue |
| George | aaaz | aaaz |
| George | P | Wake |
| Helena | E | Mudge |
| Helena | L | Kimble |
| Iain | J | Cook |

=CONCATENATE(B35," ",C35)

Function Arguments

CONCATENATE

Text1  B35          = "Bill"
Text2  " "          = " "
Text3  C35          = "C"
Text4  [ ]          = text

= "Bill C"

Joins several text strings into one text string.

Text2:  text1,text2,... are 1 to 255 text strings to be joined into a single text string and can be text strings, numbers, or single-cell references.

Formula result =  Bill C

Help on this function

OK      Cancel

**Figure 5.2** *Using the CONCATENATE formula to merge the first name and middle name*

move on to the next step. It's a laborious job, but it delivers the results. It's also a good way to highlight to your company how much time it's taking if you want them to consider a data cleansing tool!

If you have a large data set, you might find you have to repeat these steps a number of times to get to where you want if there are people in your database with multiple names. You then need to pull through these reformatted names to your main data set again. You'll be using a lookup on the original name column, so you'll need to add in two new columns – First Name and Last Name. To pull this through, as there won't be any filters on, you'll have to apply the formula to the whole column.

For the First Name VLOOKUP, the lookup value is the original Name column. You will be looking up the range from the new tab you created to split the names up, selecting all the columns, and the value that should be returned (Column Index Number) should be 2, and then 0 for an exact match – so use =VLOOKUP(original name, new tab columns, 2,0). If you don't have your first name next to your original name, it might not be a number 2 – check that you have no extra columns in there or that they are not in another order.

Next, you need to do the same for Last Name. On this occasion, it's okay to leave the formula in for the First Name as you can make them values at the same time as you do the Last Name. The lookup column will be the same, the range will be the same, and, in theory, your Column Index Number should be 3 if the previous number was a 2 and both columns are together.

Once you have copied the formula down for all the surnames, you'll need to select both First Name and Last Name columns, copy and paste special>values. Then, reapply the filters to include the new columns and check there are no sneaky N/As in there. If there are and it's a small amount, just manually correct them. If there's a lot, double-check your formula.

You could sort out the case type of the data at this stage, but I like to wait until the end as some records may disappear if they are duplicates and there's no point in running formulas over redundant data, particularly if you have a large file. Always be efficient if you can.

## Cleansing addresses in Excel

It is time to tackle the address column. This is going to be time-consuming, especially in this file and probably your own, because some of the addresses are separated by a space and some by a comma, so that is going to have an impact on the Text to Columns function.

As with the names, copy the address column into a new tab and paste it into two columns; one will be the lookup and one will be the Text to

Columns. If you already have multiple address columns in your data at this stage, I would suggest creating a new column and using a CONCATENATE formula to join all the address columns together as a lookup, and then copy this into the new tab as the lookup column.

## Commas in addresses

If you have multiple different separators in your addresses, I suggest creating a tab for each type. You might not know how many you need until you start working on it, but the usual suspects are spaces and commas. Let's start with commas. To make the process easier when pulling the data back through, in your raw data set in the first address column, run a text search on commas and only copy the addresses with commas into that tab.

Use the Text to Columns button and go through the same process as with the name, but instead of ticking the space box, choose comma. Once you've done that, apply a filter to the top row and that will show you how many columns have some data.

Rename the new columns as Address 1, 2, 3, 4 and add in a 5 if it's not there. You shouldn't need any more columns than this. Also, make sure to create these new columns in your original data set and always keep your original columns so that you have something to go back and check against if anything goes wrong.

In my sample data, working on the commas has returned four columns of data, but I know that I might need an extra address column for the addresses with spaces and so I'll keep this in mind for later when I need to pull the data back through.

When there are commas in addresses, they might only be partial, so there may be the odd address you'll need to correct manually. I would again take the approach of starting with the furthest away column, which will have the fewest number of rows.

The last column of my addresses looked good, but as I move along to the next column, this is when I need to be vigilant and look for things in the wrong place. I've used Address 5 as the dedicated postcode column and I need to move any postcodes that might be in Address 3 or 4 into Address 5. I'm going to use Address 3 as the town or city column and Address 4 as the county.

If there aren't many addresses with commas, you can just cut and paste these. If there are a lot, you might want to do an =(column with postcode) to move the postcodes into the right columns. Don't forget to change back to values.

Work through all the columns until you have your addresses formatted correctly. Now you're ready to pull these through into the main raw data set. It's important to do this now so that you don't accidentally copy them into the new tab you'll create for the addresses that are separated by spaces.

It's a similar VLOOKUP to the one that was used in Chapter 4 (see page 92) where I showed you how to pull through the different levels of classification. I've left the filter on in the address column with the commas, so instead of having to run the formula over the whole set of data, I can just do it on the selected rows. Just make sure the number of rows in the original data set matches what you copied over.

Next, put in your formula (Figure 5.3 opposite), fixing the lookup and table array values with a $, and remember to increase the Column Index number by 1 for each address column. As you have a filter on, remember to drag the formula down, not copy and paste. This will give you a nice new address format!

Once you've cleansed the comma section of the addresses, remember to remove the filter and copy and paste special>values over the formulas.

## Spaces in addresses

You're now ready to move on to sorting out the spaces. Filter out the data you've just updated by keeping the blanks and copy this into a new tab. Before you copy it over, do a quick check that it is just spaces and no other separators - if there is anything else, do them separately. Repeat the same process as with the commas by pasting two copies of the column and using Text to Columns on the second one. Put the filter on and rename the columns Address 1-5, then go through methodically, starting at the very last column and cleansing the addresses. You will most likely find that things like postcodes will get split up and you will probably have more than five columns that the data has been split out to. If this is the case, you'll need to use the CONCATENATE formula to reduce this down to fit in the five address columns.

Once that data is all cleansed - and it could take days, so be prepared! - pull it through to the main sheet using a VLOOKUP just as you did with the commas. Drag the formula down, do a quick sense check to make sure the addresses match to the original column and, when you're happy, take the filter off and paste special>values.

## Deduplication

Next, we need to think about deduplication. In this file, we could have done this step at the start because the data to be cleansed was all in the

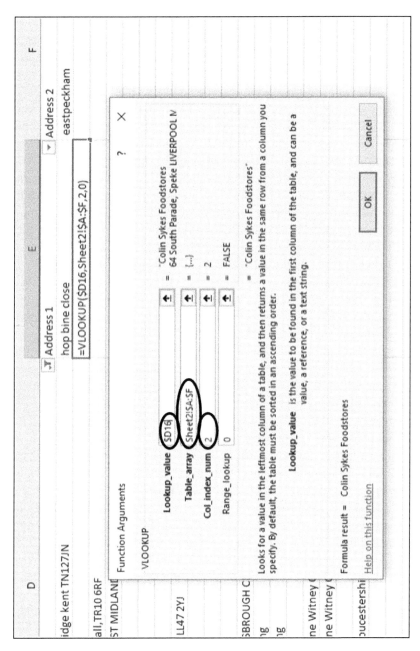

**Figure 5.3** *Using a VLOOKUP to pull through the correctly formatted addresses*

same format. However, this is very unlikely to be the case when you try this with your own data. For this reason, it's best to deduplicate at the end when everything is in the same format to make sure you can get rid of as many duplicates as possible.

As I've mentioned, you can't just deduplicate on the name. This is because you can have multiple people with the same name living at different addresses. To be extra thorough, I would recommend deduplicating on name, postal address and e-mail address. How do we do this? By using our old friend the CONCATENATE formula again!

Unlike when you were concatenating with the names and addresses and needed to have spaces between words, it's not important in this case. It's similar to the concatenate I shared with you in Chapter 4 (see page 92) when merging on the supplier name and description.

Concatenate on all name, all address fields and the e-mail address, no spaces. Once you've done this, apply conditional formatting to this column to highlight any true duplicates. If you're working in Excel, I'm not going to lie, this can be unpleasant! As you'll find out in the next chapter, I work in a different tool that helps me do this. However, in this example, we are going to do it the old-fashioned way and manually delete any duplicates. If nothing else, it will make you appreciate how lucky we are to have technology now! Start by filtering by colour on red and then sort that column alphabetically. Go through and check each line to make sure it's a duplicate that should be deleted and remove the data.

I'm very wary about deleting whole rows, so I prefer to just delete the data in the cells. For me, it feels safer. If I accidentally delete two rows of information within the cells, I can see that immediately, but if I accidentally delete two full rows, I might never notice. It helps keep things in check.

One other positive side of doing it manually – and there aren't many! – is that you really get to know and become familiar with your data, which will help for future checking and cleansing activities. Once you've been doing it for a little while, you start to notice immediately what looks right and what doesn't, which helps to speed up the process.

What about the near-duplicates? It will most likely be a name, but could also be an address. It's definitely worth checking. Firstly, create a pivot from the data and build a table with the First Name, Last Name, Address 1, 2, 3, 4, 5 *and* the e-mail, because you could have more than one customer living at the same address, such as a father and son with the same name, and that's not a duplicate. Change the pivot table to Tabular Form and remove all the Totals and Subtotals. You'll end up with a nice set of data to scroll through.

To check by name, sorting them alphabetically won't work because you might have a Robert and a Bob and they won't get picked up. The best way to do this is to sort by postcode (Address 5). Before you do that, apply an A–Z sort to the Last Name, Address 1, 2, 3, 4 and then 5 for the best layout. Then it's a case of just scrolling down and looking for those similar names and checking if they are the same customer or not.

If you want to be *extra* thorough, you can also check if there are multiple names assigned to a single e-mail. Create a new pivot with the e-mail and First Name and Last Name, make it Tabular and remove the Totals. It should then become clear where you have multiple names against an e-mail. You could use this to check for near-duplicates such as Liz or Elizabeth, or you could use this to check if multiple people are using one e-mail address, which might require further investigation.

## Formatting

Finally, you will need to tidy up the formatting, agree whether you would like to use upper case or proper case and then apply the formula =upper(select cell) or =proper(select cell). Unfortunately, you'll need to create a new formula column for each address column but it shouldn't take too long.

## Conclusion

This chapter has given you a method for the basic data cleansing of names, addresses and e-mails in Excel. It's not the easiest way, but if you need it done and are on a low budget then this is for you.

The tools from your data toolkit that will help you most in this are the Text to Columns button, CONCATENATE formula and filters. They will allow you to split out the parts of the address easily and you can then put back any extra splits by concatenating them. Generally, I'd expect you to find a mix of address formats, in which case this is when the use of filtering is also helpful.

Of course, COAT is just as applicable here. Keep those formats consistent, make sure your data is organised, get it accurate and then it will be trustworthy. It's not always easy to achieve this in Excel, so the next chapter will discuss some other ways you can classify and cleanse your data.

# 6 Other Methodologies

In the previous chapters, I've shown you how to do everything in Excel. This is because it's a widely used tool and I want to make data classification, normalisation and cleansing as simple and accessible as possible for everyone. There's no denying it, Excel isn't necessarily the easiest option! It's cumbersome, slow and open to a lot of errors, especially if you're new to using it.

## Alternative tools

There are tools other than Excel that you can use, but unfortunately many of them involve tiresome processes and still require editing of the source data separately. For example, in place of using pivot tables to check the quality and accuracy of your data, you could use a visualisation tool such as Power BI, Tableau, Qlik or one of the many others available.

Visualisation tools plug into the data source, i.e. Excel, SQL or Python. Some might help you with parts of the cleansing, but you'll still have to work in two separate tools to get the job done. This can be frustrating, time-consuming and it can be hard to trace the source of any problems.

While I try to stay as system agnostic as possible, I have only found one solution so far that gives the ability to view and edit the source data in the same window as the visualisation and update in real-time. There may be other solutions out there that I'm unaware of and I'm always looking for ways to improve my processes so I encourage you to take the methods from this book, improve on them if you can and let me know!

The more options that are available for people to work efficiently with data, the better the quality and accuracy. The most important thing for me is to get as many people working with, cleaning, classifying and normalising data as possible, however that may be.

## Omniscope

The tool that I have been working with for almost a decade is called Omniscope. From this, I have created my own proprietary methodology for efficiently and accurately normalising, classifying and cleansing data.

As with all good tools, it comes at a cost. With the projects I work on, it can shave hours, days or even weeks off of the time and can handle data in the millions of rows relatively easily. It is both a data modelling and a visualisation tool.

The one I'm going to demonstrate here is Omniscope Classic, a desktop-based version and the original tool. Why Omniscope Classic? Firstly, it's the only tool I know where I can create visualisations and have the raw data in the same view and edit in real-time. It's simply amazing. Remember the trick I showed you for working in Excel when you need to check the pivot and the raw data and you do this by adding a new window, then arranging all the views? Then having to flip between the tabs and remembering to refresh when you've updated the data? There's no more of that with Omniscope. Below, I'll take you through the normalisation, classification and checking process as I would do it, then share with you how to update and automate refreshes.

## Normalisation

The first thing that will improve data accuracy, and almost eradicate cut and paste errors, is the filters. When you 'move' or 'keep' a selection of data, there is absolutely no chance of you overwriting the data you have filtered out.

There are two ways to load your data into the software. The first is to right-click on the file you want > select Open With > Choose another app and then select the software (Figure 6.1). Whatever you do, don't tick the box, otherwise ALL of your Excel files will open like this (Figure 6.2 opposite).

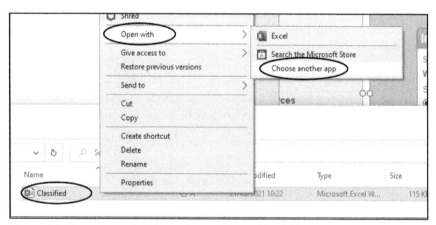

**Figure 6.1** *How to open Omniscope from a file saved in a folder*

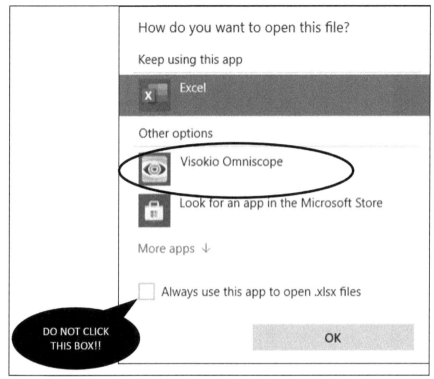

**Figure 6.2** *Selecting the right option to open the file*

As the file I'm using has multiple tabs, it will ask me how I'd like to open the file and with all or selected tabs. Choose the one(s) you need and your file will open.

Alternatively, you can open a new instance of Omniscope from your desktop and select Data Manager (this is where the modelling happens) (Figure 6.3 on the next page), drop the file in and, if like in this case there are multiple tabs, you can select the one you need (Figure 6.4). This will then pull that information through and you can load the data into Omniscope (Figure 6.5, page 115) and view it in Data Explorer (the visualisation side).

Once you've done this, you'll have a view with a chart on top and a table underneath. The way that I like to work is by changing the top chart into an aggregated table view. I do this by clicking on the top left where it says Bar and changing this to a table. I'll now have a complete mirror image of both.

I like to work with as little clutter as possible. Just as you would in Excel, hide all the columns you don't need. You can do this by clicking on the Fields box on the header of each table and selecting or deselecting the columns you need. I normally hide everything except the supplier name.

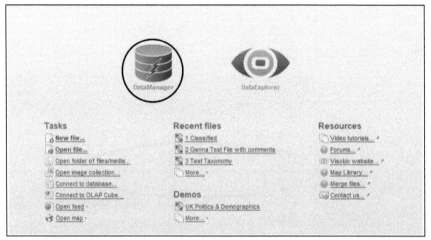

**Figure 6.3**  *How to open a file from within Omniscope*

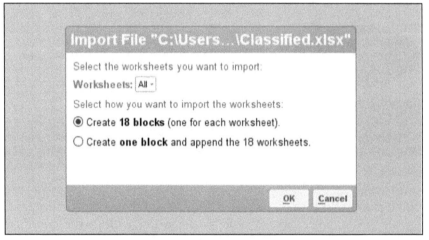

**Figure 6.4**  *Options when opening an Excel file with multiple tabs*

In the same way as using Excel, but without having to work in a new spreadsheet or tab, I create a new column (known as a field) by right-clicking the header name, selecting Tools and then selecting Insert new field (Figure 6.6 opposite). It's not a big thing, but it makes a difference – you can choose to insert the column before or after the one you clicked on. How many times in Excel have you added a column and realised it's on the wrong side and spent time deleting and reinserting the column in the right place?

Another great thing about Omniscope is that if you did happen to insert the column in the wrong place, you can easily click on the header and drag

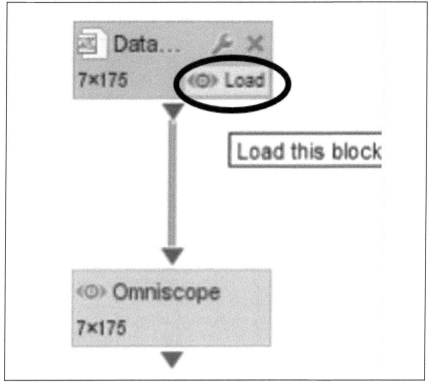

**Figure 6.5**  *Loading the block in Omniscope*

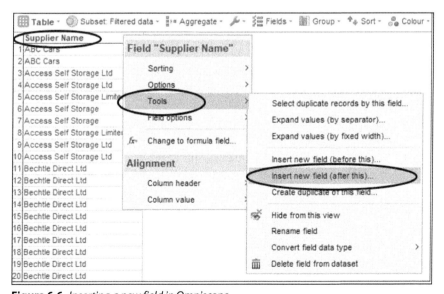

**Figure 6.6**  *Inserting a new field in Omniscope*

it to where it needs to be. You can organise the view exactly how you want it, quickly and without having to cut and paste any columns and potentially lose data.

Having created my normalised supplier column, I'll right-click to make it a formula field and enter the =UPPER(here you insert the field name from a drop-down list, rather than selecting a cell, so in this case Normalised Supplier). When the formula is correct, the text will show as green. If there's something wrong, it will be highlighted in red.

We now have everything in upper case. Just as with Excel, we need to change these to values so they can be edited. Again, right-click on the header and change to static values. Now I have this column, in the top box, I want to aggregate by the supplier name. Do this by clicking on the Aggregate button at the top and selecting Normalised Supplier. It's not needed for this exercise, but you can aggregate on multiple columns, which is very handy.

Once this table is an aggregated view, it becomes uneditable and you have to make changes in the table below. If you do try to edit it, it will soon let you know you can't. If you accidentally put an aggregation on the bottom table, you won't be able to edit that either.

Referring back to the risky and master lists in Chapter 2, you can start to remove suffixes. When you do a search and replace on the column, the great thing is that it's for that column only, so you know you are not at risk of overwriting all the columns in the file. Simply right-click on the header, go to Field Options and select Search and Replace.

As in Excel, you will have the issue that certain combinations of letters will also be part of other words, but there is an easy solution. Create a new column with the formula =RIGHT(Normalised Supplier(or name of column),3 or 4 or 5). This will give you a list of the last few letters of the word. If you remember from Chapter 2, always add in plus 1 to the number of characters delivered back so you can see if there's a space or if it's part of another word.

Two of my favourite functions in the software are the Move and Keep buttons. In this example, I've selected LTD in a cell and I'm going to click on the Keep button (Figure 6.7 opposite).

This has filtered out anything that does not contain LTD based on column Field 9. This means I can quickly check that the LTDs are genuine suffixes by scrolling down the list and, if they are all genuine, I can carry out a Search and Replace on the Normalised Supplier column.

This is great for your master list suffixes, but what about the risky list suffixes? The process is similar to the one I covered in Chapter 2, except it's far easier and quicker than using Excel. Firstly, if you have a large number of suppliers to check, scrolling and keeping is not going to be time-

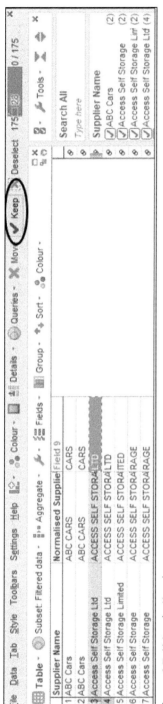

**Figure 6.7** *Using the Keep button*

efficient. This is when the search bars come in very handy. These can be found along the right-hand side. You can either Search All, which will search the whole file, or you can search by the column using the individual boxes that will be named the same as the column. For example, I have SA as a suffix and as it's a generic set of letters I know I can't just run a search and replace over the column. If I do, a lot of letters will be removed from the supplier names incorrectly. Instead, I take to the side panel and look for the Field 9 box. In there I can type 'SA' and it will pull through all the rows with SA in them (Figure 6.8 on the next page).

As you can see, there are suppliers in there that legitimately have SA at the end of their name. If there's a small number of endings that you need to remove, you can select the cell and click Move to get rid of those. If you have a lot of suppliers, the easier option might be to click Keep, for this example on just the SAs, and that will filter out anything else.

Unfortunately, if you do a Search and Replace on just the filtered rows, it applies to the whole column. So, create a new column after Field 9/your RIGHT formula column and use this to apply the changes. Unlike Excel, you can copy over the data you have filtered in without any issues as the hidden data cannot be overwritten.

Once the search and replace has been applied, you can copy that newly normalised name right back over with no need to worry about using VLOOKUPS to pull the information back through. That's all done in one file – just think how much time that's saved you.

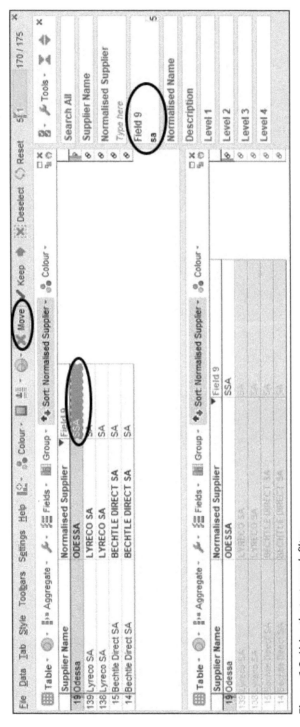

**Figure 6.8** *Using the text search filter*

You can then systematically work through the list and, when you are finished, you can delete those two columns. If you thought that saved you time, there's more! The reason the upper table is aggregated by Normalised Supplier name is that when you are finished tidying the suffixes, you can scroll down the aggregated list easily to look for near-duplicates.

Here, you can see DHL and Neopost both have multiple versions (Figure 6.9). These are common examples you might find in your own data – you wouldn't consider Express or Finance as a suffix to remove as those words are in lots of company names. Where you can save a huge amount of time is if you click on that supplier in the top aggregated view. This will highlight that supplier in the bottom editable table so you can quickly make changes.

I've highlighted in Figure 6.9 where the Supplier Name is blank; this is correct and highlights that there is more than one version of that supplier name that has been normalised to Access or Bechtle. Where the name is shown, this means that it's a unique name that is matched to that Normalised Supplier.

Another feature of aggregated tables that is useful for classification is that you can see the number of records associated with the Normalised

| | Supplier Name | Normalised Supplier |
|---|---|---|
| 2 records | ABC Cars | ABC CARS |
| 8 records | | ACCESS SELF STORAGE |
| 9 records | | BECHTLE DIRECT |
| 34 records | Brakes | BRAKES |
| 13 records | British Gas | BRITISH GAS |
| 15 records | DELL | DELL |
| 12 records | Deloitte | DELOITTE |
| 8 records | DHL | DHL |
| 10 records | DHL EXPRESS | DHL EXPRESS |
| 6 records | EUREST | EUREST |
| 6 records | EVERSHEDS SUTHERLAND | EVERSHEDS SUTHERLAND |
| 6 records | JAMES SMITH | JAMES SMITH |
| 14 records | | LYRECO |
| 2 records | Neopost Limited | NEOPOST |
| 8 records | Neopost Finance Limited | NEOPOST FINANCE |
| 10 records | Novotel | NOVOTEL |
| 1 record | Odessa | ODESSA |
| 4 records | Tele Taxis | TELE TAXIS |
| 2 records | UBER | UBER |
| 5 records | XYZ SOLICITORS | XYZ SOLICITORS |

**Figure 6.9** *Results of filtering the data*

name (Figure 6.9). This is great for building your master lists. We'll cover this in more detail later.

## Classification

With Omniscope, you can save a lot of time and improve the process of normalisation, but it really comes into its own with classification.

Imagine thousands, tens of thousands, hundreds of thousands or even millions of rows of data and some of it is misspelt or the word is cut off because of a character limit in your system. How do you find and classify this?

It's not a problem in Omniscope. By using the search boxes for either the Normalised Supplier or Descriptions, you can search for partial words and it will deliver back anything containing those words. For example, if I type in 'car rent', it will bring back anything with car rent, car rental, even rental car fuel; it doesn't have to be in a specific order. You will save so much time on searches and you can use the Move and Keep buttons to get rid of anything you don't need.

Another great example is those tricky travel descriptions – hotel parking, hotel taxi, taxi to restaurant, etc. Using Omniscope, you can easily sift through and filter out what you don't need or even add an extra word in the search box to narrow it down. This means increased accuracy, process improvements and efficient classification. If you did this in Excel, you'd have to do it description by description, line by line.

Referring back to the number of records on the left of the table (Figure 6.9), if you want to approach a file tactically, say focusing on the highest number of records by supplier first, you can find them from here. Just select the supplier you want, click Keep and you can work in that data alone.

If you want to focus on the highest spend suppliers first, it's really simple. Just sort by the value/amount column and you can keep the suppliers you want to focus on. Trying to do that in Excel would be near impossible. You could certainly find the highest value suppliers easily enough in a pivot, but how do you filter them quickly in the raw data?

When I covered normalisation in the last section, I showed you the blank cells where there was more than one supplier against that normalised name. Well, it works in other ways too. If you add in the classification columns to the aggregated view (making sure it's aggregated on Normalised Supplier only), where there are multiple classifications against that supplier, the Level 1, 2, 3 or 4 will show as blank.

However, there's a catch. If you have a mix of classified and unclassified data, the above will mislead you. Thankfully, Omniscope makes it easy to work around this: simply click on the tick in the box next to (no value) in the right-hand search pane and it will filter out any unclassified data (Figure 6.10). This will leave you with only the classified data and show a true picture of where there are multiple classifications.

For some suppliers, you would expect multiple classifications. Bechtle, Lyreco, Dell and IBM, for example, are all suppliers that provide products and services across a range of categories. If you saw a company like Eversheds with multiple classifications and you are familiar with them and knew this wasn't right, it would be obvious that they should be under Professional Services (as they are in this example). However, if you have someone working with your data who is not as familiar with suppliers, it might not always get picked up because it's not clear from the supplier's name what they do. This is why this exercise is so important, as even if the person doesn't know it should all be Professional Services/Legal Services, this process will prompt them to check the classification.

If we go back to the unclassified or part-classified suppliers, this is still a good way to potentially classify some suppliers more quickly than by just looking at all the unclassified suppliers.

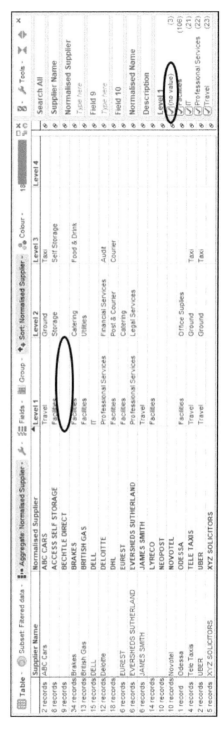

**Figure 6.10** Using the category filter

## Automation

Omniscope allows you to quickly create a master list of normalised suppliers by aggregating on the original Supplier Name (NOT the Normalised Supplier Name) and exporting that list using the little spanner icon, selecting Admin and then Export data view. It will automatically default to Excel, but you can click tabs to change this to an .IOK file, which is the Omniscope format. This is far quicker than creating a pivot, copying, pasting and then saving a new document.

We can also use the modelling side of Omniscope. Open up a new file and select Data Manager. Drop in there the file you want to normalise and the normalisation master. From the left-hand pane, select a Merge/Join box – you can either drag it or click on it and one will appear. Join the two boxes – the file you are pulling the data into should always be on the left and the file you are pulling data from should always be on the right.

There's a lot going on in this example (Figure 6.11), so I'll work from the top down to go through it. Firstly, when you drop your files into Data Manager, whether they're IOK or Excel files, it will tell you the number of rows and columns. So, the Data for normalisation file here has two columns and 175 rows. This is important because when you are merging in data, you don't want the row number to change. You might want to add in more columns, which is fine, but there's a problem if your row number changes. It's a really good check and balance way to keep an eye on your data.

Next, you need to choose the fields that you want to merge on. These could be called different things in the different files – this doesn't matter as long as you know the two columns are exactly the same in both files.

When you have matched on this, the middle row called Merged records should come back with a result. You are looking for a 'many:1' relationship and it should always be a 'many:1' match. If you have a 'many:many' result, this means you have multiple versions of the same lookup from the lookup file, which in this case is the supplier name in the master file. This could mean multiple versions of the normalised name and the merge won't work properly.

One way to resolve this would be to check the original Master Norm file and make the correction in there. If you save those changes, you won't need to re-import the file back into the model as a link has been created. All you'll need to do is press Update on the box of the file you've updated. The alternative solution is to add in a deduplicate box to the model and select to deduplicate on the Supplier Name. You can literally deduplicate at the press of a button! However, this could be risky if the wrong normalised name is removed, so use with caution.

**Figure 6.11** *Using a data model to merge files*

With a large file, you can have non-matching records from either file, which is absolutely fine unless you are expecting a full match, in which case some investigation might be needed.

Once you are happy with the match, select the columns that need to be pulled through from your lookup file, in this case the Master Norm file. In this exercise, I'm just updating the Normalised name so that's the only column I've selected. I want to tick Keep values from 'Master Norm.iok' or it will be the name of whatever file you have merged in.

A word of warning here. If you're updating normalisation for the first time (or any column for that matter), it will pull through the whole column, whatever it is called in the lookup file. However, if you already have a Normalised column, and let's say for instance it's called Normalised Supplier, you need to make sure the lookup file column is also named Normalised

Supplier. If it's not, it won't update that column, it will create a new column of the name you have in the lookup file and you'll end up with two normalisation columns with the data distributed over both of them.

There is a solution to this. Simply drop a field organiser block into the data and you can rename the field from there and run it through the model. Then you need to hit the Execute button. When that's done, the header of the block will turn yellow. You can also check from here that the number of columns and rows match the original file.

Next, you need to create an output and normalise any suppliers that did not match. Once you've normalised the new suppliers, be thorough and check the whole file - remember you may have inadvertently created some new near-duplicates.

Once that's done, if it's a new file, it's ready for classification. If this is a refresh, from here you can add in your file from master classification files. This is where the time savings really come into play.

Making a master file of the supplier name by unique classification is super easy. In the aggregated table view, which should now be aggregated by Normalised Supplier, *not* Supplier Name, select all the data. We don't want to look at any unclassified data, so remove it by unticking the (no value) in Level 1 filter, which is in the search pane on the right-hand side.

At this point, it might still be showing some blank Level 1s in the aggregated view. This is fine as some suppliers will have multiple classifications and they are legitimate. You can remove these by clicking on a blank cell at Level 1 (this has to be done in the top aggregate view) with that magic Move button.

You can then check Levels 2 and 3 and move any blanks that are multiple classifications. For example, you might have Facilities, then Cleaning, but it might separate out at Level 3 between Cleaning Supplies and Cleaning Services so it's worth checking. It's all about the detail!

As with normalisation, to map this data in, drop in the file to be classified and the master classification file. This time we want to match on normalised supplier name. Unlike last time, you will have non-matching records in your file to classify as there will only be some suppliers that have unique classifications. It's important to not only tick the merged records box, but also the one above. In this example, there are no non-matching records from the 'Data to classify' file, but it would be normal to expect some. If you don't tick the box, it could mean that you end up with fewer rows than you started with.

Always check that you have your 'many:1' relationship (Figure 6.12). This time, instead of pulling through one column, you will need to pull through all the classification columns - in this case there are four of them.

Select Keep Values and click the Execute button. Again, the bar of that block will turn yellow and it will show you the number of columns and rows. Make sure you check the number of rows remains the same.

With any remaining unclassified data, the next step would be to add in the supplier and description master file. This is created in the same way as the unique supplier, but this time you aggregate on normalised supplier *and* description. Make sure that in the Fields button you tick the Description column so that it shows in your table.

| Add join criteria |
| Which record sets do you want to retain? |
| ☑ Non-matching records from 'Data to classify.iok' (0 records) |
| ☑ Merged records (102 records, many:1) ☐ Allow many:many |
| ☐ Non-matching records from 'Supplier Classification M...' (0 records) |
| Select fields to include |
| All ▾ from 'Data to classify.iok' |
| 4 fields ▾ from 'Supplier Classification Master.iok' |
| If there are conflicting field names... |
| ○ Add new field names |
| ◉ Keep values from 'Supplier Classification Master.iok' |

**Figure 6.12** *Using the Merge/Join box*

You can then create an export file and you're ready to update your classification. This merge is slightly different in that you need to match on multiple fields/columns on both files. Remember all that tricky work creating a CONCATENATE field in both Excel sheets and then using a VLOOKUP to match them? It took as long to explain it as it did to do it. This method saves all that time.

Drop your files into the model, exactly as you would for the supplier classification master version, and connect them to a Merge/Join box. This time you need to join on multiple criteria, firstly by Normalised Supplier and then by Description. To add in an extra join, click on the Add join criteria box and select the Description columns in both drop-down menus (Figure 6.13).

Follow the same process of checking for a 'many:1' relationship, ticking both boxes, selecting the classification columns, clicking the Execute button and then checking your totals match up. When you're ready, export this data and you're ready to classify whatever is left.

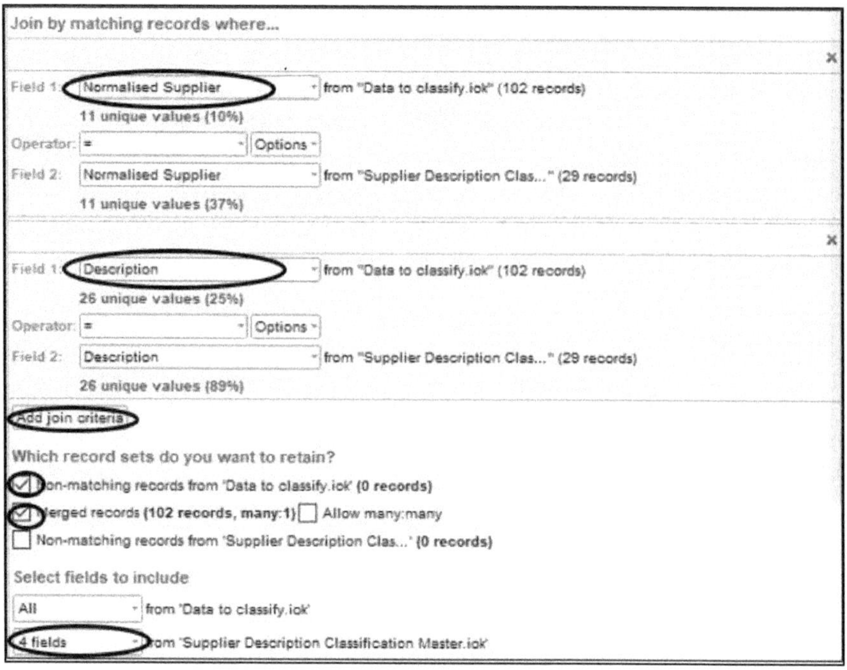

**Figure 6.13** *Using the Merge/Join box with multiple criteria*

This is a very quick explanation of my process and doesn't cover everything. I can't fit *all* my magic tricks in this book, but these instructions should demonstrate how much easier and faster it is to classify and merge data in Omniscope versus Excel, especially when you are working with large volumes of data. Not just that, it also significantly improves the accuracy of the data, which for me is one of the most important things along with consistency, organisation and trust. COAT of course!

I haven't even touched on how you can save time cleaning addresses with Omniscope. It's very much a case of using the Keep and Move boxes as you would with the filters in Excel. By aggregating the names, addresses or e-mails at the top, you can quickly spot patterns and find duplicates or near-duplicates.

## Artificial intelligence (AI), automation and machine learning (ML)

'That's great,' I hear you say, 'but can't I just let some software do it, or get someone to write some code to classify my data?'

Unfortunately not. If such an amazing product existed, there would be an industry leader with a recognised brand out there being used by all the great companies across the globe. As it currently stands, there are many different solutions providers using various different methods, scripts and rules, all trying to perfect their product. What you'll find is that even if AI, automation or ML is used for spend data classification, there will still be a team of people behind that classifying a percentage of the data and they're not always experienced in this area.

There are some great master data management (MDM) tools out there that can clean up addresses and formatting wonderfully. However, having trained tens of people in this area, I can tell you that it takes at least six months to train someone up and build up their knowledge and experience and it involves a lot of support and feedback. It's not easy – you are not working with the same type of data each project. It can be different companies, countries and industries that all have their own unique knowledge requirements.

If you do a quick Google search, you'll find numerous classification or business process outsourcing (BPO) companies in Asia, Eastern Europe and India. Why would these companies exist if everything was being automated? Plus, why would I have a business that's been running for four years providing manual classification services?

If you are being told that your data is fully automated, there's an implied assumption that it's 100% automated. If you asked the supplier what percentage of the data is actually automated, what would they tell you? Any kind of automation requires learning from, or being based on, clean, accurate data sets. How do you get those data sets? You might be able to run it through some software or write some code, but the majority of that data will need to be completed, checked, reviewed and amended by real human beings.

Even if it has been automated, it still has to be checked that it's correct and that it's learning correctly. This has to be done by humans in order to flag the errors – how would the AI know if it was wrong? If it was making decisions based on an incorrect training set, then it would think it was right. You will always need people as part of the process.

## Context

Context is something else that is extremely important in spend data classification. If we look at DHL as an example, to a professional services company they are most likely to be used for courier services; however, if a manufacturer is using the same company, they are more likely to be involved in their supply chain and providing logistics and warehousing services. If you did want to use any type of automation in this situation, it would have to know which industry the supplier is from in order to classify the data correctly. It would have to see this in several training data sets to learn and perfect this – checked and corrected by people, of course.

It's not just suppliers. Depending on how the AI/automation/ML works, it could also misread descriptions, just like the ones I covered in Chapter 4 when classifying by keywords. You could, for example, have descriptions like 'taxi from hotel to restaurant', 'hotel taxi' and 'hotel meal', which could easily be misinterpreted if not understood correctly. Automation can only learn this from the guidance of people and correct training data sets.

If you are working with a new supplier who is using automation on your data, how will they know what to classify it as, if they've never seen your data before? Yes, there will be commonalities across data sets, but a lot will be specific to your business. How will they know? Human beings are necessary for at least the first instance that the supplier is working on your data.

## The human touch

Don't get me wrong, when used correctly, AI, automation and ML are essential and valuable tools when it comes to spend data classification. They allow us to classify millions of rows of data in a fraction of the time it would take to do manually. However, this is only valuable if the data is classified correctly based on accurate training data and is checked by people. There's no way around it; manual intervention is needed for at least the training data set and checking the AI output.

There are areas where less context is involved and automation can be beneficial, such as complex items like laboratory chemicals, electronic parts or MRO supplies. What would take a considerable time for a human to research, find and classify each time, once learned by the AI can be classified at lightning speed. This is, of course, after the initial manual classification – there is just no escaping it.

The reality is that we need a mix of people and automation and you should not just rely blindly on one or the other. There is an upfront investment of time to manually classify data, but if you get it right at this stage, it will save so much time and reworks later down the line.

You can use the spot check data tips from Chapter 1 to check your own data to make sure it's as accurate as it should be. There are some clues you'll find in the data if it's been automated or semi-automated, for example, the AI or coding might randomly classify a range of suppliers and descriptions as 'construction services' when they are clearly not. This is a sign that the AI, automation or code has picked up something in its learning and has applied it widely across the data and the misclassification will appear completely illogical.

If you find errors that appear more logical, for example, you have real estate companies sitting in Facilities at Level 1 rather than at Property Level 1, or you have Travel>Subsistence>Food & Drink sitting under Catering in Facilities, then this is more likely to have been classified by a person.

We all know the tricks for making sure the top 80% of value looks good, so dig deeper into that tail spend to see what's really going on in your data and judge for yourself how thorough the automation/classification/ checking process is.

## Data cleansing tools

If you want to cleanse data such as personal information or master data, your best option might be to consider some type of data cleansing tool. There's a vast array available and I would suggest using free trials to find one that works best for you and your data. However, I would always add a word of caution about blindly trusting the software. Do spot checks, have back-ups and know your data so that if it is wrong you can spot it quickly.

## Conclusion

This takes us to the end of the alternative methodologies. There aren't many options I'm afraid and this is because spend data classification is complex work that requires attention to detail and context as a minimum.

I've shared with you some of the processes I use with Omniscope to improve efficiency and accuracy. I covered the basics of normalisation, classification and data modelling to give you an idea of the time that could be saved and how it can reduce errors.

I then touched briefly on visualisation tools. I don't think they'll be able to help you that much, but I challenge you to prove me wrong and devise your own methodology! At the very least, they will be good to help interrogate the data for errors. If you have the software already then there's no harm in using it.

Then there was the automation. While there is a place for this for certain tasks and data and it can hugely improve the time taken to complete things, it's an absolute minefield for spend data classification for all the reasons I mentioned earlier. If you do choose to go down this route, spot-check the output. If you're using a supplier, question how much of your data is being automated, ask what training data they are using and check what's hiding in the tail spend.

# 7 The Dirty Data Maturity Model

I've shared a lot of knowledge with you in this book on how to improve your spend data, but how do you know where you sit now and what needs to be improved? In this chapter, I'll introduce you to a maturity model that will help you answer those questions. Not one of those fancy consultancy models that has big words and is very technical, but one that is relatable, easy to understand and that you could give to anyone in your organisation and they would have some basic understanding of it. The inspiration for the model came from COAT.

Let me introduce you to . . .

## The dirty data maturity model

Let me share with you how you can move from dirty data to dirt-free data using this model, charting where you are, where you'd like to be and how to get there. We all want dirt-free data, but that could take years to achieve, so let's be realistic about what you have and what you could have in the next 12-24 months.

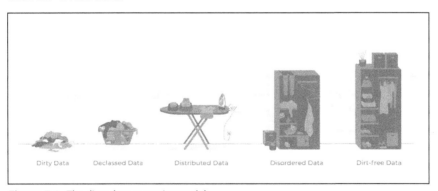

**Figure 7.1** *The dirty data maturity model*

## Dirty data

Dirty data is a pretty bad situation. It's the equivalent of turning your underwear inside out to wear it for another day – you know you have to do something about it, but you can get away with it for a little bit longer. You are delaying the inevitable. What if that one extra day you wear those underpants, you have an accident and get taken to hospital? That's when you get found out.

Data is no different. It is widely known, and I hate to say accepted, within organisations that there are data issues internally, yet no one really wants to address them. Why? Generally, it's not an easy fix, the business might not see data as an investment and the problem could be so big that there's just not the resources internally to fix it and no one wants to pay for a third party to do it. Then the data accident happens and everything gets exposed. At this point, there's no hiding from it. Fingers will be pointed, blame will be apportioned and everyone will be thinking 'why didn't we just fix this earlier?'

Hindsight is a wonderful thing. Let me help you avoid that data accident by moving you up the dirty data maturity model to minimise this risk.

Do you tick all or most of these boxes?

☐ Using Excel
☐ Multiple source systems that are not connected
☐ No type of supplier normalisation
☐ No spend data classification
☐ Never tidy or cleanse data
☐ No visibility on spend
☐ No universal systems, processes or standards in place
☐ No management or maintenance of the data
☐ No analytics or BI tools used
☐ No dedicated support or analysts.

I'm afraid to tell you that you have dirty data. You have no control over your processes, no visibility of your spend or contracts and you can't see the full picture. How do you know if you're spending too much or too little with one supplier, and in how many countries? How many suppliers per category do you have and how much are you spending per category? These are all unanswered and unknown questions in your business. You could be haemorrhaging money and have no idea.

There are certainly no standards or processes in place. You might have poorly formatted supplier addresses with information all over the place and each country or division might be doing their own thing, but you don't know because you don't have any visibility on what they are doing.

It doesn't have to be like that. To move up the maturity model, I would recommend small incremental improvements rather than drastic change.

People are creatures of habit and don't respond well to changes in routine if they've been forced on them. I would recommend involving your team, asking them what their thoughts are and how they would improve the processes. By getting them involved and taking on board their feedback, you are more likely to get their buy-in and support.

Start small. Do you have GL codes from finance you could use in the short term? You know how I feel about GL codes, but in this instance, something is better than nothing and it will give you instant visibility on where at least the majority of your spend might be sitting and with which suppliers. It could help flag some immediate areas that need addressing. Do you have parent/child organisation information from Finance that you can use in place of normalisation in the short term?

At this stage, it might be difficult to pull together all the data from your source systems unless you have some support from Finance or IT. You might have to start by working within your own system, making improvements in that, and looking to add in other systems in the future if you don't have access to them straight away.

## Declassed data

'Our data is fine; we use GL codes.' I refer you back to previous chapters discussing why this is really not a good idea! If you have just moved from dirty to declassed data, then you should accept that GL codes are not a long-term solution. You should be aiming to move up the maturity model as quickly as possible. You will find your data sitting in the declassed data category if:

☐ Using Excel
☐ Multiple source systems that are not connected
☐ Using parent/child organisation relationships for normalisation
☐ Using GL codes to manage spend in place of classification
☐ Never tidying or cleansing data
☐ Limited and vague visibility on spend
☐ No universal systems, processes or standards in place
☐ No management or maintenance of the data
☐ Analytics and visualisation in Excel
☐ No dedicated support or analysts.

At this stage, you have limited visibility on what's going on with your spend data, but it's a start. You might have a rough idea of what you're spending with your suppliers, but the GL codes could be misleading, so use them with caution. You won't be able to effectively track spend by category at this stage, but again you can look at spend by supplier or GL to get you started. Some visibility is better than no visibility, but you should be aiming for an accurate picture and GL codes cannot provide that.

You should also start to think about normalising and classifying your data. You might be considering doing this either in-house or with a third-party provider, but heed my warnings on automation from the previous chapters. If you don't know your data well enough yet, there could be a lot of incorrect classifications that you don't know are incorrect.

A great way to start getting to know your data is to classify it internally. You don't have to do all of it straightaway. Start with the top 80% of value – this will be around 20% of your data, so it will be a manageable size to classify. Try to at least get the parent/child relationships in the data before you carry out this exercise to get a more accurate picture of who your top 80% of suppliers are.

This will allow you to start making some charts and visuals in Excel, such as spend by supplier and spend by GL, which will help not only in progressing your dirt-free data journey, but also your spend analytics, contract management and cost savings journeys.

What about those unwritten rules and processes you have that everyone just 'knows'? Why not think about starting to document these so that the work can continue even if you're not there.

## Distributed data

You now have some normalised and classified data, some nice charts in Excel and an idea of what you're spending – job done. Right? Wrong. I'm afraid that if you can tick off the following, you are only halfway there:

- ☐ Using Excel
- ☐ Multiple source systems that are connected using a manual method
- ☐ Some level of normalisation but contains suffixes
- ☐ Data partially classified
- ☐ An off-the-shelf or internally built basic taxonomy
- ☐ Data is partially tidied and cleansed infrequently
- ☐ Basic visibility on spend
- ☐ Some universal systems, processes or standards in place, but not monitored
- ☐ No management or maintenance of the data
- ☐ Analytics and visualisation in Excel
- ☐ Support from Finance or IT.

At this point, you are well on your dirt-free data journey, but you're still not seeing the full picture of what's going on in your organisation as your data is siloed in multiple locations and it's not easy to pull together. It's costing you time and working in Excel means the accuracy could be compromised.

Although you still don't have a full picture of what is going on with your spend, it's more accurate because you have some normalisation in place, which will help highlight your spend by supplier. You're now classifying your data instead of using GL codes, which gives you better visibility at Level 1 across categories like Facilities, HR, IT, Professional Services and Travel.

You might have some standards and processes in place, but are you checking that these are being adhered to or are you simply trusting that they are being followed? Maybe it's time to start running spot checks to make sure.

You can start to pull charts and tables, such as spend by supplier, spend by category and number of suppliers by category. This makes a huge difference, but you're not regularly checking, updating and maintaining the data so it can quickly become inaccurate and redundant if you're not careful.

How can you progress from this stage? Try to get some dedicated support from within the business (either IT or Finance), normalise your suppliers to a higher standard based on what I've shared with you, and try applying some rules-based classification based on what you know about your suppliers and those that have a single classification, using SQL or Python, etc.

If you can, try to pull together your multiple sources of data. (This might not be something that Procurement has much influence over, it could be more of an IT decision.) It will help minimise duplication and you can start to normalise, classify, cleanse and maintain the data with consistency.

Start getting into the habit of checking and maintaining your data once in a while, as well as having a structured list of any processes and systems for the team to adhere to. It will make all the difference.

## Disordered data

We're making progress! If you are starting here, very well done to you. You are taking your data cleanliness seriously, but there are still a few things you can do to hit the pinnacle: dirt-free data.

If you've just graduated to this phase, congratulations to you too. It takes a lot of dedication and effort to get to this stage and you need support from the wider business to get here.

Consider yourself in the disordered data phase if you can tick these:

☐ Working with SQL, Python or other
☐ Multiple source systems that are connected using APIs, data warehouses or cubes
☐ Normalised suppliers to a high standard
☐ Data mostly classified
☐ An off-the-shelf or custom-built taxonomy
☐ Data is tidied and cleansed occasionally
☐ Detailed visibility on spend
☐ Universal systems, processes or standards in place, but not monitored closely
☐ Irregular management or maintenance of data
☐ Analytics and visualisation using BI tools
☐ Dedicated support from Finance or IT.

As you have suppliers normalised to a high standard and all your data is available to you in one location, it means you have a more accurate picture of how much you are spending with a single supplier. This also helps with classification as it will be easier to keep the classification of those suppliers more consistent, organised, accurate and trustworthy. Yes, COAT.

With the majority of your data classified, it will help you find even more cost savings, rationalise suppliers if needed and spot any irregular or rogue spending. Because you have some automation in place, it will also save you or your team valuable time in the classification process and increase the accuracy of the data.

You have some visualisation tools that show you great information to help with your spend journey. Charts such as top 20 suppliers by spend, spend by month, year on year comparisons on suppliers or categories, the number of suppliers by category and year on year, spend by country or division or buyer by supplier or category . . . the opportunities are endless.

How can you reach the ultimate goal of dirt-free data? It sounds near impossible, but I wouldn't give you something you couldn't achieve. Again, it's all about small incremental steps. Start by implementing regular supplier normalisation, data refreshes and maintenance. It could be monthly or quarterly depending on how much data and resource you have available, but I wouldn't leave it any longer than that.

Ensure your data is fully classified as that *will* make a difference. Once you have that, you will be familiar with your data and will be able to start applying more automation and more complex rules of classification (which in turn will save time in the classification process) and it will help cover off more classification each refresh process, meaning less manual classification each time.

Challenge the business for some dedicated resource and show them what you could achieve if you had it. You might also want to think about using a customised taxonomy at this stage so you can analyse the data the way you want to, under the categories you want.

## Dirt-free data

Let's be totally honest – there's no such thing as perfect data or dirt-free data. It might exist like that for a moment in time, but as soon as it's being used (and sometimes abused), it changes and errors creep in.

'Almost dirt-free data' doesn't sound quite as catchy, so let's go with the assumption that if you are at this level, your data is going to be as good and as accurate as it possibly can be.

Some people might be wondering why you are reading this book if you are at this level, but that is the *exact* reason why you are here. You are continually looking for ways to improve; you don't rest on your laurels or accept your data is great and leave it there. You need to keep it like that and it takes effort. A lot of hard work and effort.

If you're just joining this level, congratulations! The hard work is just beginning, but it will be worth the effort and investment. You've made it this far if:

- ☐ Working with SQL, Python or any other automation software
- ☐ Some level of AI/automation/ML
- ☐ Multiple source systems connected using APIs, data warehouses, cubes or in one system
- ☐ Fully normalised suppliers and regularly updated
- ☐ Fully classified spend data on whole data set
- ☐ Customised taxonomy used
- ☐ Data tidied and cleansed regularly
- ☐ Processes, systems and standards clearly defined, implemented and regularly monitored
- ☐ Regular data refreshes and maintenance
- ☐ Use of spend analytics and BI tools
- ☐ Dedicated Procurement analyst(s).

What does it mean at this level? You have wonderfully normalised and maintained suppliers, you have a fully classified data set that is regularly maintained and updated AND you're using some smart tools and automation to ease the workload as much as you can without compromising on accuracy.

You have a dedicated analyst or team that work to keep this data as good as it can possibly be, with the best reporting and visualisation that you need to manage your spend, monitor suppliers and feedback to the business. It's not just the classification side; your supplier information is accurate and your addresses and phone numbers are all formatted correctly to the same standard. This is all because you have implemented and are maintaining agreed processes, systems and standards.

There's nowhere better to go from here, but it's going to take a lot of dedication and commitment to stay where you are and keep that data dirt-free. Don't let your standards and processes slip and make sure any new team members are trained up properly so they can continue to maintain your high standards.

## Conclusion

Having dirt-free data is the ultimate accolade. It means your data officially has its COAT on: it's consistent, it's organised, it's accurate and therefore it's trustworthy. Establish a routine and get into good habits and you will make your workload easier. COAT really does pay off in the end.

One final note: nothing in this life, particularly data, will fall into neat, perfect buckets. You might be doing parts of all five stages of the dirty data maturity model, but it's only if you're doing *all* of the dirt-free data stage that you can say you have dirt-free data. Just because you've normalised your suppliers perfectly is not a reason to think you have dirt-free data, especially if you still have no classification and are using Excel.

Be honest with yourself and your team, challenge yourselves to do better and be better and your progression up the model will happen.

# 8 Data Horror Stories

We all like a good horror story, especially a data one. It's like when you pass an accident on the road – you can't help but slow down to have a look and then you're thankful it wasn't you. Data horror stories are just like that. It gives us comfort to know that we are not the only ones suffering and that there might be people in even worse situations out there.

This chapter will be a little bit different. Instead of just slowing down to look, I'm going to stop and help. It's inevitable that these scenarios will happen at some point so I'm going to suggest what you might be able to do if that situation occurs. You have to finish the book on a happy ending, right?

Let's start with a couple of stories that made the news.

## Scenario: Edinburgh children's hospital

There was a new £150 million children's hospital in Edinburgh, Scotland, that had to delay opening in 2019 due to a spreadsheet error from 2012. Not only did it halt the opening of the hospital, but it resulted in £16 million worth of remedial action to correct the error.

So, what happened? Well, according to BBC News, the Grant Thornton report stated:

> A spreadsheet called the 'environmental matrix' and dated from 2012 contained the 'four air changes' error for critical care. The Grant Thornton report states: 'This looks to be, based on our review, human error in copying across the four-bedded room generic ventilation criteria into the critical care room detail'. None of the independent contractors involved in the matrix picked up on the oversight.
>
> (BBC News, 2020)

When the project went out to tender in 2013, one of the bidding companies spotted the error and corrected the spreadsheet when they submitted their bid. They did not win the bid and their correction was not picked up by the team evaluating the bids. In addition to this, there was another error spotted within the same spreadsheet in 2016, but this one was not picked up *and* an independent tester also failed to pick up on these errors.

## What went wrong?

Where to start with this one?! If we go back to the origin of the error, this is where it is so important to have people with knowledge of the subject either working with or checking the data. Remember in previous chapters I've talked about spotting patterns in data? I have absolutely no knowledge of this area, but I bet if I had looked at the spreadsheet, I would have seen a trend of the same information over two columns and questioned this, especially if the information in all the other columns was also different.

There were a number of other opportunities to spot this error, particularly the bidding process where one of the bidding contractors actually flagged the error. I would suggest that if the bid team were looking at all these spreadsheets thoroughly, getting to know the data, which I have talked about many times in this book, then they would have picked up on this pretty quickly.

Again, it's down to having the right people working with the data and keeping it consistent. If you have the same person working on the data, they'll become familiar and soon spot errors.

Finally, there was another error picked up in that same spreadsheet. In my mind, if there's one error, there could be many. Wouldn't it have been sensible to check the whole spreadsheet to make sure everything looked right?

Ultimately, it seems that there was no ownership of the spreadsheet. Had this not been the case, it could have been a very different outcome, saving millions of pounds.

## Scenario: Ted Baker

Ted Baker, a clothing retailer, found a £58 million hole in the value of their inventory as it had been overstated. Initially, they thought it was a £20 million hole until new auditors came in to assess the situation.

According to AccountingWEB:

> Another concern is the highly material overstatement was apparently not identified by either management or the auditors, added Gavin Pearson, partner and forensic accountant at Quantuma.
>
> (www.accountingweb.co.uk, 2020)

## What went wrong?

COAT, COAT, COAT! I'm not a finance expert, however, I can tell you that if you were consistently checking and working with your numbers or data, then you would be familiar with them. If the numbers were to change significantly, it would stand out as a red flag for you to investigate. That would also keep your numbers or data organised, accurate and trustworthy.

Know your business! I can't believe that not one person picked up on this. There's a whole other question about data ethics if anyone were to know and chose to ignore it, but let us assume that this is ignorance. As I mentioned in Chapter 4, just as with spend data classification, don't have one person owning that data. Make sure several people work with it; it's a back-up check for the data, an extra layer of protection for fraud and it also eases the workload.

## Stories of the common data people

Let's get down to the real nitty-gritty truth about data. The things they would never publish because companies wouldn't want it getting out. I put a message out on LinkedIn for anonymous data horror stories and I wasn't disappointed. I had written most of the book by the time I put this call out, but what I couldn't believe when reading and responding to these stories was that I had already covered a lot of these issues in the book. Psychic? Not me. Coincidence? Probably not. More likely there is far more dirty data and commonly shared dirty data issues out there than I anticipated.

I am so thankful and grateful for these anonymously donated stories. Company names have been changed or removed to protect the not-so-innocent. Some stories are short, some are long, but all offer an insight into what is happening in companies across the globe right now.

### Misread descriptions

I absolutely have to start with this one, as much of the book revolves around situations like this.

> I've seen mobile yoga services categorised under telco mobile spend but then it could have been worse, it could have been mobile massage services. I'd have liked to have seen a rate card for that.

As I've shown you in Chapters 1 and 4, this can easily happen if descriptions are misread and then maintenance and spot checks are not carried out. In this case, think about context. Look at the supplier name, the description *and* the value. If it's a person's name, you'd expect a personal mobile phone cost to be around the £50 mark. You'd also expect there to be other expense charges, such as travel, associated with that supplier name. It's important to read the *whole* description. This misclassification could have happened as a result of a keyword search on 'mobile' without the data being thoroughly checked before bulk pasting the classification.

It could also have been caused by code or some form of automation. In this case, that is why final checks, spot checks and maintenance are so important. It might be a small amount misclassified now, but what about over the course of 6-12 months?

### Naming conventions

The company I work for (a huge bank that shall remain nameless), decided to migrate its data warehouse to a new Teradata platform, but doesn't appear to have involved users in the naming conventions (they aren't intuitive or follow what I've seen as best practices in naming field conventions) or verify that all fields relied upon for analysis are accounted for and mapped properly. We had some calls to discuss at a high level the project, but now I can see a big, missed opportunity to engage users. Maybe they thought they are the experts, but if the users can't understand the new fields and/or find the fields they need to do analysis, things get delayed or shot down. This is happening now. It's very frustrating.

As I said in Chapter 1, it's really important to get the whole organisation involved and this example just proves my point. How can you build and develop something for a team to use if you don't firstly find out how they are working? There could be legitimate reasons why things can't be done a certain way, but if you don't ask those people involved, you'll never know, and you might end up using them in your methodology.

This could cost your company a lot of time and money, especially if you are using external consultants. Some of the best advice you might ever get is from the people who work with the system day to day.

Remember when I spoke of the technology not working, staff losing faith in the system and going back to their old ways? This is exactly the type of situation in which this could happen.

Think also about COAT. Having a consistent naming convention is important so that everyone using the files or documents is clear on what the terms are and what they mean. Without this, you won't have organisation, accuracy or trust in the data.

### Be careful what you wish for . . .

Learnings from drop-down lists. If this data is going to be utilised to track trends or make decisions:

1  Do not have too many options
2  Do not have a miscellaneous selection

I have had two experiences where these drop-down fields are not used properly and learned that people are lazy.

One example was trying to identify root cause for service calls. In the case where there were too many options to select from, a majority of selections were the first 'alphabetical' option.

Another example was reviewing the reason for customer complaints. There were two miscellaneous type options here where a majority of complaints were categorised. This makes decisions on how to improve impossible.

I have experienced the fallout from said drop-down lists and that's how a lot of misclassification happens. People will just choose the first option, whatever that is, and you can end up with a lot of categorisation and spend classified against the item in the drop-down that begins with 'A'. This not only has an impact on categorisation but also analytics, and, in the case of customer complaints, not being able to handle them effectively.

If you think back to Chapter 3 – Taxonomies, I suggested that a good taxonomy will also reflect the quality of the data you have. Don't give people drop-down options that are not relevant to what they need to categorise, for example, 'Other', 'Miscellaneous' or 'N/A'. On the flip side, don't leave out options that they might need, otherwise it *will* end up in the wrong category.

You might have control over who inputs the information, in which case you can apply COAT to the data and make sure everyone is working to the same standards. However, if you can't control this because it's the public or your customers inputting the data, make it as easy as possible for them with clear descriptions and limited choices.

Unfortunately, there's not much I can suggest for laziness. The best I can suggest is that if it's within your organisation, get everyone involved and let them know the consequences of what happens when that drop-down isn't right. If it's the public or a customer, tell them you can't help them quickly if you don't have the right information and give them some motivation to be better.

This isn't a problem that will ever fully be solved, but we can certainly minimise the errors.

## One is never enough

I have four data horror stories for you:

1  A company wanted a CRM application with open data model and ability to add as many custom columns as they want. It finished in a messy data model with columns created with default name « column1 », « column2 » ... and the users entering any kind of data they want for their own personal use: comments, a mix of dates and text ... At the end it became a totally unmanageable database and a horror for future reports and data migration.

2  In a global CRM system of a logistics company, the documents for any loading and discharge all over the world required some information. A developer made a script for a mass update without testing it and performed the mass update in Production. The script erased some mandatory information on all customers that meant trucks and other means of transportation were not able to load or discharge goods over the world until we fixed this data horror!

3  In a data migration, a developer had a special option in a script to « clean » customer database. When executing a new batch load of migration in the morning, the developer activated by mistake this flushing option and ALL customers were deleted almost instantly in Production! Only a technical restore by DBA could solve this big horror.

4  For a telco company, there was no check on the address fields. When the assessment was performed for data migration, it was a total horror: we could see personal comments, special messages to the postman, inconsistent combinations of information (e.g. postcode vs city) ... the data cleansing on this 550,000 customer database was a horror, it took 6 months to be cleansed!

These stories were all so good and relevant to what's been discussed in this book, I just had to keep them all in and offer my solutions.

### *Story 1*

This is a classic story of data without a COAT. There are so many people involved doing things their own way that it's near impossible to maintain the consistency of the data. It's disorganised and all over the place, for example, there are probably multiple columns for the same type of information, just named slightly differently. I'd recommend having those standard agreed terms put in place, for example, date formats and units of measure.

While I'm all for having as many people involved in the discussion as possible, there are certain times when restricting editing rights is a good idea. By having a couple of people managing the file, they can field requests for new columns, which quite often could be the same requests from different people or departments. They will help maintain that consistency and organisation, keeping the data accurate and trustworthy.

## Story 2

In Chapter 1, I looked at a similar situation where if the wrong dimensions were entered into a system, the pallet loads would be incorrect and cause delays to deliveries. Deleting all the information is one sure-fire way for this to happen! How would I get around this? I would liaise with the users of the system to find out any essential/mandatory fields and make sure that these could not be overwritten without permissions. Get everyone involved.

I'd also have good back-up plans in place. I can't imagine the number of hours or days lost trying to rectify this mistake, as well as the cost to the business, including any late delivery penalties. If this was a food company then they might even have to write off fresh food. The costs could be significant.

## Story 3

Always have a back-up!! Plus, double- if not triple-check! If you didn't learn that from the previous story, then please take heed from this one. Try to put some security blocks in place so that data can't just be completely deleted without passwords or sign-off from more than one user, especially if it's essential data for the running of the business.

## Story 4

Oh dear, oh dear, oh dear. If only they had read Chapter 5 on cleansing this might not have happened. It's a great example of what I was talking about in Chapters 1 and 5 when the data is often neglected to be cleansed before a new software or system implementation because decision makers don't see the value. Well, here is an example of the hidden costs that are never considered.

There are two parts to solving this problem. The first is at the data input stage. Get that COAT on and agree standard terms, units of measure and the format of the data - what information goes in which column - and minimise this type of information from getting into the data in the first place. Have a separate comments column for this type of information so it is all stored in one location and not sent out to the customer. Imagine if it said something unpleasant about them! That's not only the cost of losing that customer but, with social media, word could spread quickly and that could also be reputational damage.

Secondly, there's the quality assurance (QA) stage. This is your spot-checking and maintenance step and this is the perfect example of why it's a vital part of the process. Have dedicated team members working on this part of the process if you can. If they are familiar with it, they'll soon spot when things don't look right and correct them.

If this took six months to fix, can you imagine the business interruption that would cause? If your team is trained properly and has the right tools, they could fix it much more quickly. It's not all about the problem, it's also about how you handle it.

### The shapes that don't go together

I had a project where I had to check, summarise, synthetise, analyse and visualise the monthly 'planned vs actual status' of a metric for 4 months, within 30 factories of the company, situated in different countries. Besides the 'planned vs actually used' concept, which caused some confusion because in some places they did not have a plan, every single factory sent these numbers in a different format, in a different Excel solution, even though I had sent them a template file. They completely disregarded that template.

More often than not, me and my team leader had to beg them to send the data. We were pressured by the regional VPs and other big position holders within the company to do it. To make things worse, I was the only employee who was responsible for 'department data' so I had no help. My team leader (who managed another team of different focus besides me) was mainly there to micromanage me (never done it before, only for the sake of this project).

This resulted in a huge backlog of regular tasks, because my team leader was so hell-bent on satisfying the VPs that I had to drop everything else whenever a new Excel file came in. Some of these files were in languages neither of us spoke, so we could not figure out the meaning of the columns without Google Translate. When we asked the plant/factory if we can have an English version of the report, their response was: 'this is how our 20-year-old system can pull the data, so deal with it'.

We did not have any database management system or cloud solution, all I had at my disposal was MS Excel. Halfway around the project the VPs wanted changes retrospectively by excluding certain elements. This resulted in endless VLOOKUPs in approximately 45 files. The final straw was when my team leader came up with the idea to make a safety-check system to see if the calculations and the numbers are accurate. The project was a success after all, but me and my TL ended up hating each other and I quit right after the project ended.

This is an example of when language, country and culture come into play and why it's really important to get the whole organisation involved, or at least the key stakeholders if you can. Think of it this way: when you work in a factory you really don't care about filling a spreadsheet with some numbers that mean nothing to you, for someone halfway across the world. If you knew that it would help save you time with your workload in the future, save costs for your factory or even affect your own bonus, might you be a little bit more interested? If you're in an office, you might not understand what it's like working in a factory where there's no time to stop and fill out spreadsheets. Maybe some of the people you are requesting the information from are not very IT literate and are therefore struggling. Plus, there's the potential language barrier on top. If you can get everyone in a meeting, it could help ease the tension and improve the situation.

Spreadsheet templates DO NOT work, however hard you try. You are forcing the person who is providing the information to sit and fill in a form that could be open to misinterpretation, especially if there's no COAT on the data. It's just not going to happen; they have their own priorities and this will get left. A more successful way to get the information you need would be to build a template with two tabs - one for how you would like to view the data, order, format, etc., and one for pasting the raw data into and pulling through to the other tab. You can then pull together all the correct tabs into one spreadsheet at the end. This would also hopefully help with the VLOOKUP problem with the 45 files that was faced at the end of the project.

With this approach, you will need a template for each different format and this can be done in Excel. Quite honestly, if you're working on a project like this, you'll be lucky just to get the data on time so try and take the brunt of the workload if you can. Once you have this all set up, it should be easy enough to update this on a monthly basis, which will make your life easier and also help manage those regular tasks better.

In terms of the language issues, there might not be an easy solution. From experience, I would say that you'll see the same things repeated each month, so you might be able to translate the descriptions then use them as a mapping in future files. If it was based on product code, you could spend the upfront time translating the information, knowing that you could map it for each future monthly update. This is of course in a perfect world and we know that is a rarity! In this situation, the reality is that some hard spreadsheet hours will also be needed.

## Don't lie to me
When the CMO basically tells you to make the data match the story she's been telling. Highly unethical.

This is short but packs a punch. I couldn't leave this story out as I'm sure this happens a lot more than people are willing to talk about. In this particular case, it's for marketing, but it's still fraud or deception at the very least. In other areas of business, such as finance, you could end up in jail for these actions. In my world, it's a firm and unmovable 'NO'. I will not compromise the integrity of the data for anyone, even myself.

It's a tricky situation to be in when you have to work with these people. My advice would always be to keep the data, and yourself, true. There is always a path back to the truth, even if you try to hide it. It could cost you your job, your career or more. Is it really worth it?

There is also a bigger question to ask yourself about whether you really want to work in a company where this is acceptable.

## Driving you mad

In 2002, I had just taken over a Data & Analytics team at (a well-known motoring company). Its parent company was building a massive cross brand data warehouse for analytics and CRM. It took another year after it was supposedly finished to finish testing and migration of reporting, analytics and campaign selections.

One month, soon after going live, we started getting feedback from Marketing that customers were complaining of getting mail for other customers. After a mail house investigation, it appeared the latest copy of the data mart for selections had suffered from a cartesian join and mixed-up names and addresses. Although pre-GDPR, there was no PII arguably in the mailing for motor and home insurance.

A few of us spent time fixing the data mart and giving fix files to the mail house but it was too late, most of the mailings had left and arrived on doorsteps. Back then we lived in the world of cross charging and Marketing tried to 'sue' the data team for the mistake for not only the wasted mailing cost of £150k but also lost revenue of £200k. We didn't even have a budget other than for people, so it was a silly idea.

I did some campaign analysis of the 75% of customers who had received a mailing for someone else at their address (although it was their renewal month) and they had responded and bought at 80% of the normal rate (last month/same month last year and the 25% who we fixed). So it showed perhaps the mailings didn't really work and people would have bought anyway as it was their renewal month and didn't care about the wrongly addressed mailing. Marketing dropped its decision to 'sue' us.

Since then, I have employed all sorts of checks and balances on data warehouses and specifically the CRM files that go to mailing or emailing. Just because it ran without error doesn't mean it's right.

I love this story because there is so much to learn from it and it's such a positive example of how to deal with a messy problem. Firstly, it's all about checks, balances and maintenance. An eyeball spot check of some of this data could have flagged an issue and, as the contributor writes, just because it ran without error doesn't mean it's right. Never take anything for granted and this is true in many aspects of data. I believe that as good as technology is, sometimes a good old-fashioned human eye is the most effective tool you can use. It's free, all it will cost you is some time and it is your last line of defence in dirty data. The story is also a great example of what I said earlier about it not being what the problem is, but how you deal with it. They tried to fix the data and get it to the mailing house before it went out. When only some of it did and the rest didn't work, they didn't give up – they were proactive and did analytics on the mail that *did* go out and got some amazing insights that might never have been discovered.

This ties in nicely with communication. At the start, there wasn't a great relationship between the marketing and data departments and perhaps this wouldn't have been as big an issue if marketing had been involved at an earlier stage. Things changed when the data team shared their insights with the marketing team and proved their worth. They fought their corner and won and hopefully that relationship continued to improve. We shouldn't have departments trying to 'sue' each other; a collaborative approach is much more effective.

## Final thoughts

Perhaps some of you are shaking your heads and disagreeing with me and thinking that there are better solutions to these problems. Of course there are, but most involve some kind of financial investment and most decision makers or budget holders are not willing to pay out for this. There are many people out there who are having to struggle and make do and, for them, I hope my suggestions make a difference.

You will have noticed that there are recurring themes in my responses. If you take away any advice from this chapter it would be:

Get that data COAT on. Especially the consistency part. If you can get agreed standards amongst your colleagues, this is a huge step in the right direction and organisation, accuracy and trust will follow. And never fudge the numbers.

Communication is key. Have a meeting, build a relationship, explain why you need the information you do and the impact it will have. Don't just demand it in an e-mail. Work collaboratively with your colleagues to find a better solution.

Also, there's spot-checking and maintenance. This is incredibly important as a catch net for things that have been missed in previous steps.

It could save so much more than the hours of checking involved - think of the costs to the business, reputation and time spent/wasted.

Finally, have people who know the data working with the data. It helps catch errors, they will be more efficient at the work if they know the data well and accuracy will increase, ultimately reducing the number of errors. This advice takes us to the end of our journey. It's been a pleasure to share my knowledge with you. If you need a recap of everything we've covered on this wild dirty data journey, you'll find it in the next chapter.

# Summary

We've covered a lot in this book, so it is helpful to summarise and pull together the main points.

I hope you've enjoyed reading this book and have been able to take something away from it to improve your data quality. I've certainly enjoyed writing it - a lot more than I thought I would! - and I have really surprised myself with how much I can actually write about data. There's another tip for you: even if you think you can't - try! You'll be amazed at what you're capable of.

The same goes with data normalisation, classification and cleansing. You might think it's a mammoth task and that it's too big to deal with, but you can start small by focusing on the high value spend or customers or the most frequently used data and work from there.

## Dirty data

I've shared with you the types of dirty data you might find, and of course, there will be some specific examples related to your organisation. But in general, it will be things like: misspelt names, incorrect or misleading descriptions, missing or incorrect codes, no standard formatting of addresses or units of measure, currency issues, incorrect or partially classified spend data, and not forgetting the most popular, the duplicates.

In terms of the consequences of dirty data, I've given examples of what could go wrong and what has gone wrong for some of my clients in the past. Fear not though, you now have spot-checking tips for your data toolbelt.

## COAT

What goes better with your data toolbelt than your data COAT? Your data needs to be consistent, organised, accurate and trustworthy and you have to have all four as they are all interdependent. Make COAT fun so that you can engage non-data people within your organisation in a meaningful way and relate it to any data situation.

## Normalisation

When you're ready to add to your data toolbelt, you can start to normalise your suppliers. The key message here is 'rinse and repeat' – don't just normalise once and think that's it. As you are cleaning up the data, you can create new near-duplicates that need to be tidied up, so go back and check a second or third time. Use the risky and master lists in the book to guide your normalisation. It will help you work more efficiently and accurately and who doesn't want that?

## Taxonomies

Once your data is perfectly normalised, you can then build up your data toolbelt further and classify your data more efficiently with the customised taxonomy you've built. You might want to take smaller steps and start with something off-the-shelf, but think about your long-term objectives – a customised taxonomy could be more suitable.

You can begin with a template and the one I've given as an example is a great start. You need to build it to fit the needs of the business as you are classifying the data, being consistent, appropriate, suitable and relevant. Finally, it has to be analytics friendly, so think about how those categories will translate onto the screen as a chart.

## Data classification

I've explained best practices for classifying your data: how to classify, how to update refreshes and how to create and update master classification files. That's everything you need to keep your data updated and accurate.

The most important thing to remember is that context is everything. If you're only working with a section of the data, you aren't seeing the full picture. Think about 'who am I classifying for?' and 'would this company buy this product or service?' and this will keep you on the right track. It might not come easily or naturally at first, but with practice and regular use, it does improve.

## Data cleansing

It's not all about the spend data; there are other types of data too and so I covered basic data cleansing of addresses and e-mails. In general, you can expect to have various different formats for addresses, possibly from multiple systems. The best thing to do is use Text to Columns for any addresses that are in a single cell and then work with the filters to cleanse anything else.

It's a lengthy process, but it will get you familiar with your data. Don't forget that when dealing with personal data, wherever you are based, always work with the basic principles of only acting on your documented instructions, don't contract a sub-processor without prior approval and delete or return all personal data at the end of the contract. Be sensible, keep it secure and don't share it with anyone.

## Data tools

If you think that normalising, classifying or cleansing data in Excel is just too hard, consider other tools for the job, such as Omniscope. You might think that the cost prohibits you, but the time saved just improving the process is worth it, especially if you're working with large data sets. There are a number of visualisation tools you might be able to use and apply the methodology I've shown you. You have to find something that works for you - create your own new processes with these tools and write your own book; nothing is stopping you!

If you're considering the AI/automation/ML route, I've provided you with tips to manage your expectations on what can be achieved with technology. Firstly, you need good, clean, accurate data sets to learn from and if you're being told your classified data is automated, why not check and ask 'what percentage?' You might be surprised by the answer. Spot-check that data and make sure it's accurate to a level you're happy with. Don't just check the top 80% of suppliers, dig a bit deeper and see what you can find in the tail spend.

## Data maintenance

All these efforts will be in vain if you don't maintain your data regularly, whatever type it is. Work out how often it needs to be maintained based on the volume of data and the needs of the business. Make it a habit, block it out in your calendar, do whatever helps you make this part of your routine.

## And, of course, the horror stories

I finished up the book with some data horror stories. I'm sure some of you were taken back to your own experiences of data nightmares and I hope that if you were to have any again (hopefully not) you will have picked up some tips from my suggestions. It's always easy to look back with hindsight, but if you've prepared for the unexpected by keeping your data as clean as possible, that's half the battle.

I can't leave you without saying it just one more time: get and keep that data COAT on!

# References

Accelerated Insight (2021) *Spend Analysis: What is Spend Data Classification,* www.accelerated-insight.com/spend-analysis/what-is-spend-data-classification

AccountingWeb (2020) *Ted Baker Admits to £58m Hole as Stock Count Error Doubles,* www.accountingweb.co.uk/business/finance-strategy/ted-baker-admits-to-ps58m-hole-as-stock-count-error-doubles

BBC (2020) *Spreadsheet Error Led to Edinburgh Hospital Opening Delay,* www.bbc.co.uk/news/uk-scotland-edinburgh-east-fife-53893101

CIPS (2021) *What is the Tail Spend in Procurement?,* www.cips.org/knowledge/procurement-topics-and-skills/operations-management/managing-the-tail

Collins Dictionary (2021) *Definition of 'Taxonomy',* www.collinsdictionary.com/dictionary/english/taxonomy

Deloitte (2019) *The Deloitte Global CPO Survey 2019,* www2.deloitte.com/be/en/pages/ strategy-operations/articles/global-cpo-survey-2019.html

DLA Piper (2021) *DLA Piper GDPR Fines and Data Breach Survey: January 2021,* www.dlapiper.com/en/uk/insights/publications/2021/01/dla-piper-gdpr-fines-and-data-breach-survey-2021

Harvard Business Review (2018) *Artificial Intelligence for the Real World,* https://hbr.org/2018/01/artificial-intelligence-for-the-real-world

Technopedia (2021) *What Does Data Classification Mean?,* www.techopedia.com/definition/13779/data-classification

The Guardian (2021) UK Digital Skills Shortage Risks Covid Recovery as Young People Shun IT Courses, www.theguardian.com/business/2021/mar/21/uk-digital-skills-shortage-risks-covid-recovery-as-young-people-shun-it-courses

Wikipedia (2021) *Artificial Intelligence,* https://en.wikipedia.org/wiki/Artificial_intelligence

# Index

accuracy 11–12, 16, 22, 51, 63, 87,
111–12, 120, 126, 129, 135–6, 138,
142, 149–50
  data 21, 33–4, 63, 112
AI (Artificial Intelligence) 10–11, 16, 18,
126–8, 137, 153
  *see also* machine learning

category tree *see* taxonomy
Chartered Institute of Procurement &
Supply (CIPS) 8
charts 25, 40, 134–6
classification 1–3, 6–7, 9–12, 15, 23–4,
28, 33, 38, 61–8, 69–80, 82–86,
88–92, 94, 97–8, 99, 106, 111–12,
119–21, 124–5, 127–9, 132, 135–8,
141–2, 151–2
  best practice 70, 152
classified 2–3, 5, 7–9, 11–12, 16–18, 23,
25, 29, 33–4, 40, 63–4, 66, 70–1, 73,
75, 78–9, 82, 86, 89–90, 93–4,
120–1, 124, 128–9, 134, 136–7, 143,
151, 153
classify 2, 8, 10, 14, 17, 24, 39–40, 61–4,
66–8, 72–5, 78, 82, 86, 89–90, 97–8,
109, 120–1, 124–6, 128, 134–5, 152
classifying 11, 14, 40, 61–2, 67, 69–72,
74–6, 79, 88–9, 98, 111, 127–8,
134–5, 152–3
cleanse 47, 92, 109, 129, 132, 135, 153
cleansed 34, 99, 106, 134, 136–7, 144–5
cleansing 56, 99, 101, 104–6, 108–9, 111,
129, 133, 144–5, 151–3
  addresses 104
  names 99
COAT (Consistent Organised Accurate
Trustworthy) 16–17, 19, 24, 34, 40,
51, 65, 67, 70–1, 74, 78–9, 82, 92,
98–9, 109, 126, 131, 136, 138, 140,
142–5, 147, 149, 151, 154
cost savings 7–8, 14, 18, 67, 74–5, 134,
136
currency 4, 7, 18, 34, 66, 151
cut and paste 1, 12–13, 15, 23, 47, 49, 82,
94, 102, 105, 112, 116

data cleansing tools 129
data dictionaries 14
data dictionary *see* data dictionaries
data governance 14
data protection 1, 13, 19–22
  *see also* GDPR
deceptive descriptions 6, 82
declassed data 133
deduplicate 107–8, 122
deduplication 106
dirt-free data 131, 134–8
dirty data 1, 5, 9, 17–18, 29, 34, 62,
70–2, 131–2, 138, 141, 149–50, 151
  consequences 5, 9
dirty data maturity model 131–2, 138
disordered data 135–6
distributed data 134
duplicate 3, 5–6, 13, 18, 34, 38, 108
duplicates 4–5, 9, 14, 42, 54, 59, 99, 101,
104, 107–8, 124, 126, 151
duplication 7, 15, 135
duplications 4

Excel 1, 15, 23, 39, 45–7, 57, 75, 90, 94,
99, 101, 104, 108–9, 111–14, 116–17,
120, 122, 125–6, 132–5, 138, 146–7,
153

function 45, 54, 75, 97, 104
  CONCATENATE 90, 92, 94–5, 102–3,
    105–6, 108–9, 125
  COUNTIF 90–1, 94, 97
  RIGHT 46–7, 50–1, 116–17
  Text to Columns 101, 104–6, 109, 152
  TRIM 45, 54
  UPPER 42–3, 58–9, 116
  VLOOKUP 45, 56–9, 90–4, 96, 104,
    106–7, 117, 125, 146–7

GDPR 1, 19–22, 148
  see also data protection
General Data Protection Regulation see
  GDPR
general ledger (GL) codes see GL codes
GL code 62–3, 74–5, 89
GL codes 3, 62–3, 74–5, 133–5

Information Commissioner's Office
  (ICO) 20–2

machine learning (ML) 126–8, 137, 153
maintenance 15, 29, 34, 132–4, 136–7,
  141–2, 145, 148–9, 153
master search list 46, 51–2
maverick spend see tail spend
misclassification 2, 65, 68, 79, 129,
  142–3

near-duplicates 4–5, 42, 54, 59, 108–9,
  119, 124, 126, 152
normalisation 9–10, 12, 37, 37–40, 42,
  56–9, 75, 99, 111–12, 120, 122–4,
  129, 132–6, 151–2
  automation 57
  best practice 42
  in Excel 45
normalised supplier 41–2, 45–6, 51, 53,
  57–8, 71–3, 75, 79, 86, 90, 92, 97,
  116, 119–20, 122–5
normalised suppliers 41, 53–4, 59, 90,
  122, 136–7

Omniscope 111–15, 120, 122, 126, 129,
  153

parent/child relationship 39, 133–4
pivot table 23–8, 33–5, 53, 56–9, 90, 97,
  108
Power BI 111

Qlik 111

risky list 42, 46–7, 116
Robotic Process Automation (RPA) 10
rogue spend see tail spend

search engines 87–8
software 9, 12, 18, 38–9, 112, 116,
  126–7, 129, 137, 145
spend tree see taxonomy
spot check 15–16, 22, 33, 128
spot checked 14
spot checking 15, 22–3, 29, 34, 75, 149,
  151
spot checks 1, 15, 72, 90, 97, 129, 135,
  141–2
standardisation see normalisation
supplier rationalisation 6, 40

Tableau 111
tail spend 8–9, 129, 153
taxonomy 61–8, 69, 75, 86, 92, 134,
  136–7, 143, 152
  custom 66, 136, 144
  customised 67, 75, 137, 152
  how to build 67
  off-the-shelf 66–7, 75, 134, 136, 152

units of measure 4, 7, 17–18, 34, 144–5,
  151
un-normalised suppliers 41